To Sue
Be happy
Barbara Eubanks

Humorous Happenings in Holy Places

101 ANECDOTES & DEVOTIONALS

BY BARBARA EUBANKS

TATE PUBLISHING, LLC

Published in the United States of America
By TATE PUBLISHING, LLC

Book Design by TATE PUBLISHING, LLC.

Printed in the United States of America by
TATE PUBLISHING, LLC
127 East Trade Center Terrace
Mustang, OK 73064
(888) 361-9473

Publisher's Cataloging in Publication

Eubanks, Barbara

Humorous Happenings in Holy Places/ Barbara Eubanks

Originally published in Mustang,OK:TATE PUBLISHING:2004

1. Humor 2. Devotionals

ISBN 1-9331481-9-5 $13.95

First Printing: December 2004

DEDICATION

*To my three sons and my eight grandchildren
who have truly been a fountain of
humorous happenings for my writing*

*To my dad who taught me to enjoy life and to main-
tain a sense of humor through all circumstances*

*And to my loving husband who has always been
my encourager, enabler, and the love of my life*

*If there be any glory or if there be an praise,
may it go to our Heavenly Father.*

TABLE OF CONTENTS

From the Mouths of Children

Music Makes the Heart Merry

Country Church Memories

FOREWORD

When you connect humor with faith, it makes for joyful, entertaining, and enriching reading. In *Humorous Happenings in Holy Places,* I marvel at how Barbara Eubanks, a pastor's wife, has captured the funniest people blunders and has turned them into spiritual gems for thought and application.

What follows in these pages are 101 stories that will bring a smile to your face, tickle your funny bone, and cause you to laugh out loud. And who doesn't need that? You'll love reading about the crusty sinner man, now a new convert, who startles his country church with his prayer. As a PK (preacher's kid), I especially like the country church pew stories about funeral mistakes, elderly folks snafus, pulpit slip-ups, church crises, baptisms, wrong words but the right meanings, a real shotgun wedding, and those priceless children's Christmas play mishaps.

The book begins with the innocent words and actions of children, both Barbara's own and those in her husband's various pastorates. As children take things literally, laughter many times follows, and it does here.

Holy places do produce laughter, like when a bird flies into church and perches on a good sister's Sunday hat. Barbara takes those unforgettable happenings and shapes them into purposeful spiritual truths that call for faith in action. Every story of laughter follows with pertinent scripture verses and passages which enlighten and enliven our everyday Christian example and witness.

Barbara's focus on humor in spiritual terms speaks volumes about her own faith and how the spirit of Christ flows freely through her. How she integrates laughter and faith speaks highly of her writing craft, and the reading will be pleasing to your heart and spirit.

I venture to commend Barbara's book for moments of amusement and nourishment for the soul. If you want to laugh and be blessed, start reading.

Wayne Atcheson, business manager
Jerry B. Jenkins Christian Writers Guild
Colorado Springs

Introduction

"Our mouths were filled with laughter, our tongues with songs of joy . . ." Psalm 126:2.

In a world plagued with sorrow and troubles, the Word of the Lord and our daily devotions should be a source of peace, comfort, and laughter. Proverbs 15:13 reminds us "A happy heart makes the face cheerful, but heartache crushes the spirit."

Therefore, if we Christians are to be conduits of God's joy and peace, it is important that our spirits are restored with cheer and laughter. To that end, I purpose this book of serious but light-hearted, and hopefully even funny, daily devotional moments. The anecdotes are from true church and religious-related experiences that my husband as pastor and I as his helpmate have collected over the last thirty-plus years in the ministry.

FROM THE MOUTHS OF CHILDREN

He called a little child and had him stand among them. And he said: "I tell you the truth, unless you change and become like little children, you will never enter the kingdom of heaven. Therefore, whoever humbles himself like this child is the greatest in the kingdom of heaven. And whoever welcomes a little child like this in my name welcomes me."

Matthew 18:2-5

I.

Do You Hear Him Call Your Name?

When our second granddaughter Hannah was about two, her parents took her to "big church" with them one Sunday night, as they often did. She was very well-behaved and normally entertained herself with the toys from her "do" bag. She appeared to be preoccupied with her Barbie dolls and oblivious to the preacher as he read the scriptures and called many names of those involved in the passage.

The pastor read from I Samuel 1 about Hannah's weeping and failing to eat because she was barren and about praying God would give her a child. He continued the sermon regarding God's faithfulness to answer sincere prayers and his answer to Hannah with her conception of Samuel. Dramatically he emphasized, "When Hannah cried out to the Lord—"

Suddenly Hannah's ears perked up and her attention was drawn from her play. She looked up to her mother and exclaimed, "Mommy, Hannah not crying."

Names are just as important to each of us today as they were to people in Samuel's day. Even though we may share the same name with another person, we know with a certainty that when our parents call our names, they are talking to us, and no one else. We should be as sensitive to the call of our Heavenly Father. God knows our name because He is our Father, and when He calls us to service, we must answer.

Jesus emphasized this when he said, *"Why do you call me, 'Lord, Lord' and do not do what I say? I will show you what he is like who comes to me and hears my words and puts them into practice."* Luke 6:46-47

Read I Samuel 1 and 2 for an understanding of God's faithfulness and care for His children and to see how Hannah responded to His goodness to her.

Pray that your ears will be sensitive to God's call and that your heart will be eager to answer and respond.

2.

Don't Worship Those Idols!

As we were going down the walk of my cousin's lake house, my five-year-old granddaughter Alicia frantically started saying, "Gram, Gram, don't look! Don't look!"

I asked, "Don't look at what?"

She excitedly answered, "Don't look at that idol. The Bible says not to look upon idols."

I, then, discovered a small, concrete garden ornament in the flowerbed. I realized that in Alicia's eyes, it was an idol.

We are to be as cautious and urgent as my granddaughter in keeping idols, or anything else (save the one true God) from our lives, that would become a source of worship.

God's instructions to His people were very explicit in this matter. He reminded the people of His goodness and deliverance of them and that they were to have no other gods before Him. This same edict applies to us today. Often man forgets God's protection and provisions for him and, in turn, gives credit to lesser things.

Do not turn to idols or make gods of cast metal for yourselves. I am the Lord your God. Leviticus 19:4

Read Exodus 20:1-17.

Pray that God will put a shield around your heart that keeps out anything that would take your eyes off of Him or that would in any sense become an idol for you.

3.

Don't Be the Pinball

My surgeon son was recently invited to speak to the Christian Medical and Dental Society. Since his duties take him away from his family so often, he asked them to accompany him that night so that they could all be together.

He based his talk on a Dr. Seuss book, *Places You Will Go*. He acknowledged that through the intern and residency years, most of doctors' time and steps are dictated by their trainers, patients, and by the training process itself. He emphasized that just as they knew then who and what controlled their lives, they, now, should recognize just as plainly who was directing their lives, where they were going, and what they were doing in life even after their time in medical school. He emphasized that they shouldn't be swayed by every demand on their time, but that they should, instead, make sure that God was the controlling force behind their lives. He said, "You shouldn't just bounce around like a ball in a pinball machine."

On the way home his daughters, ages nine and thirteen, were praising their dad for his good speech. Sandy, his wife, tested their understanding and asked them what meaning they got from it. They reiterated what he had said almost verbatim. She then asked Austin, their six-year-old son. He thoughtfully replied, "Well, I think what he was saying was that if you play pinball, don't be the ball."

Too often in life we are, indeed, the pinball being knocked to and fro, not even aware of the forces propelling us. Often, we let life's demands and circumstances consume us instead of our enjoying the abundant life that Christ promises. God should truly be the controller of our lives.

. . . I have come that they may have life, and have it to the full. John 10:10

Read John 10:1-18 and be reminded that it is God's will that you, as his child, have an abundant life and that He be in control of your life.

Pray today that God will keep you from being knocked to and fro by stresses and pressures in your life and that He will help you to discern the direction He wants you to go.

4.

God is in the Control

Children have a definite concept about whom and what should be in authority over them. My grandson Austin is the youngest in his family and his two older sisters tend to tell him what to do quite often. It's okay with him for his oldest sister to dictate to him because there are several years that separate them in age, however he resents the younger sister trying to boss him. When he was three, his favorite thing to say to her was "You are not in control; God is in **the** control."

He had a young friend who had a different notion about God and control. The friend had heard his parents talking about the remote control and later about God controlling their lives, but he understood things differently. When his mom, checking his understanding of God, asked him where God was, he picked up the TV remote control and said, "God is in the control."

God should be in control of our remote controls considering the trash that enters many homes

through TV, but more importantly, we should surrender complete control of all areas of our lives to him.

*My eyes are ever on the LORD, for only he
will release my feet from the snare. Psalm 25:15*

Read Matthew 7:24-29.

As you pray today, surrender everything in
your life to the authority of the one who created
you.

5.

If Roy Rogers Had Been There

One of my friends tells about his brother's reaction to the crucifixion account. He grew up in the era of Western movies. One Easter his pastor painted a vivid word picture in his sermon about the cruelties that Jesus suffered during his trials and crucifixion at the hands of his enemies. This young boy was intensely interested. He became so absorbed in this story that he forgot himself and spoke out, "If Roy Rogers had been there he would have shot them!"

Have you heard the crucifixion story so often that it has just become another story, or do you feel the anguish of Jesus anew each time you hear it? May we all be indignant toward the persecutions that Christ endured for our sakes and, therefore, live our lives in constant thanksgiving for his sacrifice for us.

Read this account in Mark 15.

He told them, "This is what is written: The Christ will suffer and rise from the dead on the third day . . ." Luke 24:46

In praying today, thank Christ anew for His

sacrifice and suffering for your salvation. Recommit your life as a living sacrifice for Him.

6.

Dead People in There

During Vacation Bible School one summer, the pastor was giving the five-year-old class a tour of the church. As they passed the baptistery curtain, one child was overheard telling another, "Don't look in there. There's a bunch of dead people in there."

It took the pastor a short while before he realized why the child said that. He remembered the phrases that he used during each baptism service. "We are dead unto sin and buried with Christ in baptism."

Perhaps the child has a more accurate understanding than do most adults. Baptism is a beautiful symbol. When we are baptized, we symbolically say that we die to ourselves, are buried with Christ, and are resurrected to live for Him. This is a public declaration of a private commitment to the Lord.

For me, to live is Christ and to die is gain.
Philippians 1:21

Read Paul's philosophy concerning life and death in Philippians 1:13-30.

Humorous Happenings in Holy Places

Pray that you will die to self daily and let Christ live through you.

7.

Big Green Jesus

Soon after my husband had accepted a new pastorate, he preached one of his "sugar stick" sermons (sermons pastors keep on file to use over and again because they have previously been well-received or well-liked.) This particular one is one of my favorites because of an illustration he uses in it: He tells that the writer of the hymn "Victory in Jesus," E.M. Bartlett, and his wife used to sing the hymn in the car as they traveled from church to church. She eventually became terminally ill and was in and out of a coma. As he was by her bedside as she was dying, she weakly motioned for him to lift the oxygen tent. When he did, she began singing in a soft, trembling voice, "I heard an old, old story . . ." Her husband listened as she sang a few more words. Then her life slipped away. Her grown children were reflecting on this sweet memory before her funeral. One commented, "Isn't it a shame that Mother didn't get to finish the song?" Her father replied, "Not really; although she began it here as a solo, one day soon, we will finish it as a duet in heaven."

As one church family was driving home after the service the day my husband preached that sermon, the parents were discussing the new preacher and how much they liked him and his sermon. Their nine-year-old daughter chimed in and said, "I like him, too, but I've never heard that song 'Big Green Jesus' ('Victory in Jesus') that he talked about."

Just as the child misunderstood the song title, many Christians know the song but miss the meaning of it in their daily lives by failing to claim God's victory over their circumstances. We can have victory over our fears and struggles in life through Jesus Christ.

For everyone born of God overcomes the world. This is the victory that has overcome the world, even our faith. I John 5:4

Read I Corinthians 15:50-58.

Name and thank God today for all of life's victories that have been yours because of Him.

8.

No Time for Baths

Children tell it like it is, especially during
"children's time" on Sunday mornings. [Children's
time is a time when the minister calls the children
to the front of the church, sits with them in a circle,
and does an interactive lesson or sermon for them as
part of the regular Sunday morning worship service.
The congregation looks on and listens to this (and
seems to enjoy it), even though it is directed toward
the children.] As the children interact with the pastor,
they often reveal their families' secrets inadvertently.
So was the case when my husband was trying to
explain that we should be clean on the inside just as
we are outwardly. He told the children, "I know all of
you had a bath before you came to church this morning if you didn't get one last night." One little fellow, who was from a family with five boys, quickly
blurted out, "I didn't get a bath. My mommy said we
didn't have time for everybody to bathe, and I was
the least dirty." It was easy to detect whose child he

was because his mother sat red-faced in the front row of the choir.

We live in a time and place where most people have very little trouble getting their bodies clean. Soap and water are plentiful. Our concern should be that we are also clean within. God's grace and forgiveness are just as readily available as soap and water. All we must do is call on Him. He can and will cleanse us from all unrighteousness if we will repent and ask for forgiveness.

Create in me a pure heart, O God, and renew a steadfast spirit within me. Psalm 51:10

Continue to read all of Psalm 51.

Pray today that God will cleanse you from all unrighteousness and will make you a vessel worthy of His use.

What do
Elephants
and Cars
have in common?

9.

How are a Car and an Elephant Alike?

Another "children's time" that proved to be disastrous was the occasion when my husband asked, "How are a car and an elephant alike?" He was attempting to make the point that they both had trunks in which to store things and that it is important that we store the word of God in our minds and hearts.

Without hesitation, a brave young boy offered rather loudly, "They both have gas."

God's word is a great treasure to be stored in the hearts of his children. When it is there, it guards our hearts, souls, minds, and bodies against the snares of worldly lusts and temptations. It also renews our faith and strength in times of doubt and trouble.

I have hidden your word in my heart that I might not sin against you. Psalm 119:11
Read Psalm 119:9-16.

Humorous Happenings in Holy Places

Pray that you will have the ability to read and remember scriptures and hide them in your heart so that they will come to you as you need them.

10.

Not into Religious Stuff

When Dane, one of our grandsons, was four years old, his parents thought that a new children's Bible would be a really great Christmas present for him. He excitedly tore into each of his presents and would spend time playing with each one until he opened his nice, new Bible. He simply looked at it, put it down, and went on opening other presents. Later his mom asked him, "Don't you like your new Bible?"

"I'm just not too much into that religious stuff," he candidly replied. Actually, he normally was very much into "religious stuff"—his Sunday School class, his daily prayers, and his family devotions.

Many adults really aren't "too much into religious stuff"; they just aren't as open and honest about it as children tend to be. Often we, as adults, aren't anymore discerning about what is truly valuable in life than was this four-year-old. We fall into society's trap that says, "Work, work, work so you can buy your children more, more, more." Actually spending quality time with your children is so much more valuable than buying them more things, just as genuine faith is so much more valuable than gold.

These have come so that your faith—of greater worth than gold, which perishes even though refined by fire—may be proved genuine and may result in praise, glory, and honor when Jesus Christ is revealed. I Peter 1:7

Read Matthew 6:19-34 to determine the things of true value. See how many things are mentioned in these verses that should be held in high esteem.

Pray that God would reset your priorities so that only those things of spiritual value are first in your life.

11.

I Want to Go Live with Jesus

When she was only three-years-old, Alicia, our oldest granddaughter, was staying with us for an extended visit while her parents were in Europe. Every night of her visit, she and I would recount the day's fun and blessings when I tucked her in and then we would pray together. One night after our ritual, she looked up at me, smiled and said, "Gram, I want to go to heaven and live with Jesus."

I replied, "Someday, you will, Darling, when you are much older."

Surprisingly, she corrected me and said, "No, I mean I want to go tonight."

Perhaps out of shock or perhaps out of a faith that paled in comparison with hers, I answered, "Well, you can't go tonight. What would I tell your parents when they call? You'll have to wait until Jesus gets ready for you."

As I lay in bed that night, I pondered her request and my reply. To begin with, I felt an uneasiness and wondered if she had some kind of premonition that she was about to die. I finally realized that the reason Alicia had said that she wanted to go to Heaven and live with Jesus was not because she thought she was about to die but rather because she had heard in church about the beauties and wonders of heaven and that when people died, they went to live with Jesus. She simply believed these truths. It is this childlike faith to which the Bible refers in Mark 10:15. I prayed that night thanking God for her faith and asked for a renewal of that pure, unadulterated childlike faith in my own life which she had exhibited.

Matthew 6:30 reminds us of the importance of faith in God. It says *"If that is how God clothes the grass of the field, which is here today and tomorrow is thrown into the fire, will he not much more clothe you, O you of little faith?"*

Read how God instructs us to become like children in Matthew 18:1-11.

Pray that you will become like a little child as you approach God. If you have never accepted Christ as Savior, today, come in childlike faith and enter His kingdom.

12.

No Toys in Heaven?

Probably one of the most pondered questions is "What will heaven be like?" Children who grow up in church hear about heaven all their lives but sometimes manage to get an off-center view of what it will be like. My young grandson Austin was spending some time with us one summer. He had a young friend visiting with him one day, and as we were driving home, I heard their discussion about heaven. Austin said, "Heaven will be boring. There won't be any toys there." His friend echoed that sentiment.

I inserted, "Why do you guys think heaven will be boring?"

Austin answered, "Oh, there will just be adult stuff to do there."

"What kind of stuff?" I questioned.

"You know, writing papers and talking on the phone and stuff like that."

Feeling it necessary to dissuade him from a dread of heaven, I borrowed a philosophy that a dear pastor friend had used with his son. I told Austin, "If it takes toys in heaven for you to be happy there, then there will be toys."

This is my true belief—whatever it takes for us to experience ultimate bliss in heaven, God will provide. I just believe we will live in such a superior realm to what we live in now that we can't comprehend the joys that God has in store for us.

Praise be to the God and Father of our Lord Jesus Christ, who has blessed us in the heavenly realms with every spiritual blessing in Christ. Ephesians 1:3

Read II Peter 3:11-18.

Pray that your faith will be strengthened to truly believe that God will take care of you both in this world and the next and that any fear or dread of death will be removed from your mind.

13.

I Want to be Advertised, too

When our oldest son was seven, our visiting evangelist was extending the invitation one Sunday. No one had made a move. To our dismay, Steve, Jr. stuck one hand in his suit pocket and started sauntering toward the front of the church. My husband, who was at the front to receive new members or to counsel with those who came forward, saw him first. He gave him that special "I'll discuss this with you when we get home, boy," look because he thought our son had chosen this inopportune time to go out the door near the altar to the bathroom.

Instead, much to both his dad's and my surprise and pleasure, he walked up, took the evangelist's hand, and made a very mature profession of faith. He also decided that morning that he wanted to follow the Lord in baptism.

The extended family received this news with much excitement, and all wanted to attend his baptism the following Sunday. Our middle son Scott observed carefully the attention that Steve received and the delight he brought the grandparents with his conversion. The amount of attention focused on his older brother was just about more than he could take.

On our way to the baptismal service, Scott exclaimed from the back seat, "Daddy, I want to get 'advertised,' too, 'cause I'm just as good as Steve." And truly he was, but it was a few years later before Scott understood that it is not man's goodness that buys salvation, but rather God's sacrifice through His son.

For it is by grace you have been saved, through faith—and this not from yourselves, it is the gift of God—Ephesians 2:8

Read all of Ephesians 2.

Thank God that, although your goodness is insufficient for salvation, His goodness covers all your sins.

14.

When You Eat This Bread
(or Chiclets, as the case may be)

It was in his first year as a pastor and probably his first time to conduct The Lord's Supper service when my husband almost lost his composure. The small country church we pastored had no nursery; therefore, my primary activity during services was to try to prevent our three little boys from disturbing worship, which was no minor undertaking. On the night my husband conducted his first Communion service, believing that I was being creative and avoiding numerous questions during that very reverent time, I gave Scott, our four-year-old, a Chiclet to put in his mouth while the bread was being served. He closely observed me and his older brother taking the bread and holding it between our fingers, waiting for the appropriate time to eat the bread. He held his Chiclet just as we held our bread. My husband looked out at the congregation and said,

"When you eat this bread, do it in remembrance of me," and then he put the bread in his mouth. When he did, Scott caught his eye as he, very reverently, put his Chiclet in his mouth. A repressed grin eased across my husband's face, which broke the solemnity of the service. Others had followed his gaze and had also observed Scott's imitation observance.

I know God has a sense of humor and probably smiled as He looked down upon the child as well. But, he does not smile at mature Christians when they take the Lord's Supper in an unworthy manner. Christians are admonished in I Corinthians 11:27-29 to examine their lives and are warned that taking the Lord's Supper without recognizing the body of the Lord is a sin against the body and blood of Jesus Christ. I Corinthians 11:30 even cautions that taking the Lord's Supper in an unworthy manner may result in weakness and sickness. Therefore, we should ask God's forgiveness for the sin in our lives that makes us unworthy. We should take the bread and wine in remembrance of who He is and what He has done for us.

I (Jesus) am the bread of life. John 6:48

Read about the first Lord's Supper in Luke 22:1-23.

Pray that, not only during the observance of the Lord's Supper, but every time you eat a piece of bread that you will remember Christ's sacrifice for you.

15.

I'm Bored

The renowned psychologist and humorist, Charles Lowery, was once our guest revival speaker, at the church where my husband served as associate pastor. Our pastor's six-year-old son spent so much time at church that he was easily bored and often expressed this to his parents.

On that particular night, he came out of his church training class, walked up on the stage, sat down by his dad (or rather the person who he thought was his dad), leaned over, put his head on him and said, "I'm bored."

Charles Lowery, whom the lad had mistaken for his dad, replied, "Well, son, I've heard that complaint before, but never before the service even started."

Many adults get bored in church. Often we, as adults, grow weary in the ritualistic attendance of so many services and forget to count our freedom to worship as a blessing from God. When the joy of attending worship services becomes drudgery, perhaps that is all we are doing—attending and not worshipping.

Galatians 6:9 instructs us, *"Let us not become weary in doing good, for at the proper time we will reap a harvest if we do not give up."*

Read Galatians 6.

Pray that God will renew your strength, your joy in worship, and your vision for well doing.

16.

What's in the Glass?

During "children's time" one Sunday morning, my husband, in trying to teach the children "faith is the evidence of things unseen," used an object lesson. He held up an empty glass and asked the children if they could tell him what was in it. No one could. Then, to give a hint, he put the glass to his nose and sniffed deeply. An angelic little girl blurted out, "I know, I know! It's snot!"

That ended the children's sermon that day because my husband couldn't continue above the roar of laughter from the congregation.

We adults need to be reminded that without faith our salvation is impossible. We must also remember that faith is essential for Christian daily living and for answered prayers. The Bible teaches, if we pray believing, God will hear our prayers and will meet our needs. Hebrews chapter 11 chronicles the work of faith in the lives of many Biblical characters.

*Now faith is being sure of what we hope for
and certain of what we do not see. Hebrews 11:1*

Read in Hebrews 11, the chapter known as
the "hall of faith," about the ways God has worked in
His children's lives as a result of their believing.

Pray that you can have faith as strong as those
who are named in this "hall of faith."

17.

Just Say "WOW"

Bethany, one of our young granddaughters, was spending a few days with us. As usual, we tried to find activities to make her visit a memorable one. We rode the horse, went swimming, had friends come to play, went to McDonald's, and did many other interesting things. When bedtime came, I took her upstairs to say prayers and to tuck her in. I asked if she would like to pray aloud. She responded, "Gram, let's just do wow prayers tonight." When I told her that I wasn't sure of what a "wow prayer" was, she told me, "You just name the good things that God has done and the good things that have happened that day and then say, "Wow, God!"

She then began to name the fun-filled activities of the day and the people who are special in her life. After recounting each one, she would say, "Wow, God!" With this, I learned a new way to genuinely praise God. For the beauty of this world, for His ever-abiding presence, for His continued mercy, grace, and forgiveness, and for giving us His son, I say "Wow, God!"

Then a voice came from the throne, saying: "Praise our God, all you his servants, you who fear him, both small and great!" Revelation 19:5

Read other verses encouraging praise: Psalm 22:25, 45:17, 65:1, 67:3, 71:6, 89:5, 119:164, and 150:6.

Try doing "wow prayers" of your own today. Name the good things in your life and then say, "Wow, God!" after each one.

18.

Mama Said We'd Have to Go to Church

When our grandsons Zack and Reagan came to spend a few days with us one time, they enjoyed some good, old-fashioned, grandparent spoiling. Their days and nights were filled with lots of activities, and their normal bedtime was ignored. We stayed up late, watched television, and played games. On Saturday night I told them that we needed to get to bed a bit earlier than we had been, for the next day we would be getting up to go to Sunday School and "big church." Reagan, the younger of the two replied with resignation, "Yeah, I knew it. Mama said we'd have to go to church when we came to your house."

"Of course we do," I responded, and we did. (I am glad to say that this is now also the routine in their home.)

Both Reagan and Zack made new friends and enjoyed the experience much more than they anticipated. Although children sometimes dread the confines of Sunday clothes and the strictures of staying still awhile, they soon learn to say with David, "I rejoiced with those who said to me, 'Let us go to the house of the LORD.'" Psalm 122:1

Read Psalm 127.

Pray that you will be made glad each time you enter the Lord's house to worship. Also, pray that God will give you the wisdom to pass on this joy as a heritage to your children and grandchildren.

19.

Please Not Today, Dear Jesus

While my sister and her family were living in Texas, they attended a large Baptist church that had numerous night meetings. One particular week, during a revival, my sister attended service every night, leaving her toddler in the church nursery.

Later the next week, she was running some errands and was stopped at the traffic light in front of the church. Young Marc, who had just begun making sentences, saw the church and from the back seat said, "P-l-e-a-s-e, dear Jesus, not again today."

While some may spend so much time at church that they secretly feel what Marc expressed, there are many others who rarely see the need of church attendance. What would our lives be like if we were denied the opportunity of going to the Lord's house to worship? We take this privilege too lightly. John tells us of the kind of worship that pleases God.

Yet a time is coming and has now come when the true worshipers will worship the Father in spirit and truth, for they are the kind of worshipers the Father seeks. John 4:23

Read about the importance of group worship in Acts 2:41-47.

Pray that your attitude will be one of joy when you enter God's house to worship and that you will worship in spirit and in truth.

20.

Boots or Bible

When my daughter-in-law read a book to Dane, my grandson, about a boy who wanted a new pair of red rubber boots, he was introduced to a new word—or so she thought. In one place in the story, the book referred to the boots as galoshes. To improve his vocabulary, she always discussed the meaning of new words with him. She asked, "Dane, have you ever heard that word; do you know what it means?"

After pondering a moment, he responded, "Yeah, I think I have. Doesn't that come right after II Corinthians?"

Although he was a bit off target, I thank God for parents who take seriously the instruction to "Train up a child in the way he should go." Without that training, my grandson would not have known the books of the Bible (with any pronunciation).

Train a child in the way he should go, and when he is old he will not turn from it. Proverbs 22:6

Read Proverbs 22 in its entirety.

Pray for parents who try to abide by this instruction and that God will give them wisdom to teach their children the precepts that He would have them to teach.

21.

Time's Up!

Some friends of ours were in church one Sunday when at exactly 12:00 noon a very loud alarm clock sounded. The young pastor turned pale because the deacons had already expressed to him that people were tiring of his long sermons. To the parents' dismay (and later to the pastor's relief) they discovered that the clock was in their young daughter's purse. After they turned it off and the service ended, they questioned her as to why she had her alarm clock with her. She replied, "Daddy always says that the preacher doesn't know when to stop, so I thought I would remind him." Now what could a daddy say to that!

Perhaps an alarm clock won't sound, but we need to constantly be reminded that in an instant, our time can be up. Death is not prejudiced; it comes to both young and old, to both rich and poor, and to both Christians and non-believers. We should live each day as though our last alarm is about to sound. If you knew this was your last day on this earth, what changes would you make? To whom would you apologize? Or what good deed would you do that you have you been delaying?

. . . It is not for you to know the times or dates the Father has set by his own authority. Acts 1:7

Read Acts 1:1-11.

Pray today that you will live each day with the expectation of Christ's return.

22.

Out of the Mouths of Babes

Often adults pray for things which sound "churchy;" however, children pray for any and everything. A friend of ours, who is a minister of music, raised his family in a house near a pasture. At night, he and his wife would go into their children's bedrooms for prayer time where each, in turn, would say a nightly prayer. The youngest child got caught up in the "bless everybody" routine. After naming everybody he could think of, he started naming things. Thinking he had said the last amen, the parents started to leave the room just as he interjected, "And, God, bless the cows and the cow patties."

We adults should praise God in all things and for all things. If we name and enumerate our possessions and blessings, our hearts will overflow with gratitude to God. It does wonders for us to list these things, for it reminds us that we came into this world with nothing and that everything we possess is a blessing from God. Just as we like for our children to acknowledge the gifts we give them, our Heavenly

Father is pleased when we concede that we are nothing and have nothing without Him.

Every good and perfect gift is from above, coming down from the Father of the heavenly lights, who does not change like shifting shadows. James 1:17

Read I Chronicles 16:29-36.

Thank God for all His blessings toward you and your family; name them one by one. Thank Him even for those that you can't name.

23.

The Good Things

Having raised three sons, my husband and I often found ourselves in the role of referee or arbitrator as they were growing up. Arguments ensued over choice seats at the table, in the car, and over any other location for which our boys could compete.

I tended to extinguish one flash fire, only to have another flare up over something else. My husband, the wiser parent, sought a more permanent solution for these chronic debates. He said, "There are three of you and seven days in the week; therefore, each of you will get the pick of all these prized things two days each week. That leaves one day extra. Whoever calls it first on Sunday morning gets 'all the good things' that day."

Thereafter, early every Sunday a shout from one of the boys would awaken us; "I get all the good things today." That day, that early bird would enjoy all those dear privileges.

Every time I enjoy that fond memory, it reminds me that, as Christians, we have "all the good things" every day if we but recognize them and know that all good things come from above. How blessed we are to have an abundance of food, good shelter, closets of clothes, pure water to drink, good friends, freedom to worship, and the list goes on and on. It also calls to mind, my very favorite life verse:

Finally, brothers, whatever is true, whatever is noble, whatever is right, whatever is pure, whatever is lovely, whatever is admirable—if anything is excellent or praiseworthy—think about such things. Philippians 4:8

Read Philippians 4:8-12.

Pray that your eyes will be opened to see all the good things God has brought into your life; then acknowledge and thank Him for them.

24.

There are Ghosts Among Us

While my husband was attending Southwestern Theological Seminary, he and I had the opportunity of co-teaching a four-year old Sunday School class. Our church's successful bus ministry brought in many children. Often one of the little boys would crawl up onto my husband's lap while he was teaching the Bible story.

On a Sunday following Halloween, he said, "Many of you dressed up as ghosts and goblins on Halloween, but none of us really believe in ghosts, do we?"

A beautiful little blonde-haired boy, who was sitting in his lap, looked up at him innocently and said, "My daddy believes in ghosts."

"Oh, really?" questioned my astonished husband.

"Yes," replied the four-year-old. "He believes in the Holy Ghost."

Quickly my husband corrected himself and said, "Oh, I believe in that Ghost too."

Thanks to Jesus' death, burial, and resurrection, the Holy Ghost can be with people throughout the world at the same time, without bodily restraints. It is so very important that we are sensitive to His presence in our lives.

Again Jesus said, "Peace be with you! As the Father has sent me, I am sending you." And with that he breathed on them and said, "Receive the Holy Spirit." John 20:21-22

Read John 20.

Pray that you will always be aware of the presence of the Holy Ghost in your life and that this knowledge will make you aware of the power you have at hand to handle life's circumstances.

25.

A Child Shall Lead Them

Our oldest granddaughter Alicia has always been a very religious child. When she was very young, two or three, she would stand on the curb by the apartment where her family lived, raise her hands, and sing praise songs that she composed to the Lord. We knew then that she was likely to have an evangelistic nature.

When her sister Bethany came along, she had a less serious nature and was truly a free spirit. Alicia often worried about Bethany's misbehavior and her sins. This became an even greater concern after Alicia made her profession of faith at age eight. She even expressed to her parents that she was afraid Bethany would die and go to Hell. Apparently, she felt that she, like the Philippian jailer, should see to it that all of her family was saved.

One night, my son and his wife noticed that the children were being unusually quiet and were out of sight. That usually meant trouble. They started to the stairs to go up and check things out, but before they reached the hallway, they heard a mumbling. They listened more carefully and sneaked a peek, only to find Alicia in the foyer with her little sister (who was only three at the time) on their knees, with faces to the floor. Alicia was having Bethany repeat the sinners' prayer after her. Bethany thought it was a game and was doing her best to follow her sister's lead, but Alicia's heart was pure in trying to bring her little sister to a saving knowledge of Christ. She was afraid that Bethany would die having not experienced Jesus' saving grace. Oh, that each of us would be so vigilant in bringing the lost to Jesus!

They replied, "Believe in the Lord Jesus, and you will be saved—you and your household." Acts 16:31

Read about the jailer's conversion, followed by that of his family in Acts 16.

Today, pray that God will renew that evangelistic spirit in you so that you will seek out lost family members and bring them to Christ.

26.

Join Hairs with Jesus

My granddaughter Hannah has beautiful, thick, flowing hair, which is her pride and joy. One Sunday morning the congregation sang "Family of God" as the fellowship hymn at the close of the service. Hannah had been unusually quiet on the way home. Looking rather puzzled, she later came into the kitchen while her mom prepared lunch. Her mom asked her what was wrong. She asked, "Mom, why would we want to join hairs with Jesus?"

It took her mother awhile to comprehend where she was coming from with that question. Then she remembered the words to the song " . . . *joint heirs* with Jesus, as we travel this plod, for I'm part of the family, the family of God."

This incident draws to mind the story of the sinful woman who brought perfume to anoint the feet of Jesus and wiped her tears from his feet with her hair. Her humility and willingness to make this generous sacrifice pleased Jesus. Our hearts should be so overflowing with praise that we cannot help but to pour out generous sacrifices in praise to our Father.

. . . and as she stood behind him at his feet weeping, she began to wet his feet with her tears. Then she wiped them with her hair, kissed them and poured perfume on them. Luke 7:38

Read this story in Luke 7:36-39.

Pray that you will recognize your sins, as this sinful woman did, and follow her example of humbleness as you approach Jesus in prayer.

27.

Guess I Can Have Some of That Grape Juice Now

When our grandson Dane was six, he started asking his mom and dad questions about going to heaven and receiving salvation. They answered truthfully and simply so he would be satisfied. One night after he turned seven, he told Tracy, his mom, that he needed to pray and ask Jesus to come into his heart because he just had a funny feeling in his stomach.

After counseling with him, Tracy and Dane knelt together, and, indeed, he did pray to receive Christ. Scott, his dad, was at work at the tire plant at the time. Dane could only contain his excitement and joy about his salvation for so long, so shortly thereafter he and his mom called Scott at work to tell him the good news.

Dane told Scott what he had done that night. After Scott expressed his pleasure in his son's salvation, Dane asked, "Daddy, I guess that means I can have some of that grape juice and those crackers now, huh?"

With amusement Scott agreed that indeed Dane would get to participate in the next celebration of the Lord's Supper. As the entire family will remember forever Dane's honest comment, hopefully, he will remember the blood that Christ shed for his salvation each time he takes "that grape juice and those crackers."

In the same way, after supper he took the cup, saying, "This cup is the new covenant in my blood; do this, whenever you drink it, in remembrance of me." I Corinthians 11:25

Read I Corinthians 11:23-34.

Pray that Christ will renew the joy of your salvation that you experienced when you were first saved and that He will draw to your remembrance His ultimate sacrifice which made your salvation possible.

28.

Guess I Can Ride My Bicycle Now

Our grandson Dane has always been just a step ahead of his parents. His thinking seems to be on another level than theirs. After his conversion experience, he asked his dad, "Guess I can ride my bike to school now that I'm saved, huh?"

"Well no, Son. It is five miles to school and the road is still just as curvy and dangerous as it was before. Besides, you are just seven-years-old."

"But Daddy, if I get killed now, it won't matter because I'll be going to heaven."

How wonderful to have the simple trust and assurance like that child! Maybe as adults we should rest more fully in the promise of eternal life, not so that we may live reckless, foolish lives, but so that we may live lives with the peace of knowing that even though many perils may take our bodies, nothing can take our souls except Jesus Christ himself.

. . . and free those who all their lives were held in slavery by their fear of death. Hebrews 2:15
Read I Corinthians 15.

Pray that doubt and fears in your life will be replaced by ultimate peace, knowing that God has secured your future through Christ Jesus.

29.

Hut One, Two, Three

Children have a way of bringing every day life into their prayers in a very natural way. With them, there is no pretense. Whatever is on their minds and hearts comes right out of their mouths when they pray. So it was when my nephew Dolph said the blessing over his lunch when he was about three years old.

At the time, he had been in the yard playing football with some older friends. His mom called him in for lunch. She reminded him to say the blessing, so in keeping with his day, he bowed his head and began, "Hut one, two, three. God is great, God is good . . ."

In football terms, God certainly scores a touchdown with his perpetual goodness toward us. His greatness is represented in his wonderful creations—the mighty oceans, the highest mountains, and the endless sky.

How great is your goodness, which you have stored up for those who fear you, which you bestow

*in the sight of men on those who take refuge in you.
Psalm 31:19*

Read more about the goodness and greatness of God in Psalm 33.

Thank God for His goodness toward you as you pray today.

30.

Shut Up and Pray for Something Else

Children who grow up in church usually reach an age when they willingly share their concerns and whatever is on their minds with their age group classes. Such was the case on a Sunday night when the teacher of a four and five-year-old class asked if anyone would be willing to say a prayer. One little boy always seemed to volunteer. This night he prayed, "Dear Lord, please help Gracie's finger to get well."

Gracie, his little sister, punched him and disgustedly exclaimed, "Ah, shut up and pray for something else; my finger is already well."

Although his prayer was not received well by his little sister, I know God heard his prayer and hears ours as well. Not only does God hear our prayers, He answers them also. Apparently He answered that one posthaste. If we approach Christ with an innocent, childlike spirit, He will never tell us to shut up and pray for something else.

When I was a child, I talked like a child, I thought like a child, I reasoned like a child. When I became a man, I put childish ways behind me. I Corinthians 13:11

Read I Corinthians 13:9-13.

Pray today for the children in your circle of acquaintances. Many of them may not only have physical problems, but may have emotional concerns as well.

31.

Spend Time with the Lord

One of the Godliest women I have ever known gave her time every year to teach in Vacation Bible School. During her last summer to volunteer, her daughter-in-law and granddaughter were both in town visiting, so her granddaughter went with her to Bible school and was in her class. On Wednesday she was to present the Bible story of Mary and Martha. The lady carefully taught the children that while Martha was frustrated with Mary because she wasn't helping her prepare the meal, Mary was doing the more important thing—spending time with Jesus.

When they returned home, as the lady was preparing lunch, the phone was ringing, and there were knocks at the door. The lady became more and more frustrated as she couldn't get lunch on the table due to all of the many hindrances. As her annoyance began to show more and more, her granddaughter upbraided her, "Grandmother, I think you need to just spend more time with the Lord."

Sometimes it is easier to teach Bible stories than it is to live out their lessons.

"Martha, Martha," the Lord answered, "you are worried and upset about many things, but only one thing is needed . . ." Luke 10:41-42

Read God's instructions in Luke 10:38-42 about what we should place as the priority in our lives.

Pray that God will give you the discernment to distinguish between what is good and what is best when you prioritize your time.

32.

What Do We Say Every Night

My beautician told me that her son and his wife were trying to strictly train up their three-year-old child in the way he should go. They took a very active approach in his spiritual training. They took him to Sunday School, read Bible stories to him, always had him help say the blessing at meal time, and had bedtime prayers. They were very pleased with his involvement in these things and wanted their parents to be aware of how well they were doing with his training.

One night they took their son to visit his grandparents (my beautician and her husband). The young dad coached, "Jason, tell Grandmother what we say every night."

The little fellow held up his finger, shook it in a scolding manner, and replied, "Don't you get out of that bed!"

Certainly, that was neither the desired nor the expected response of the parents, but it was a truthful answer.

Their instructions to their son were in direct contrast to what Jesus told the paralytic whom he healed. Keeping children in bed at night time can be a challenge, but to get a paralyzed man up walking was no challenge for Jesus. All he had to do was speak the words and the man was healed.

I tell you, get up, take your mat and go home. Mark 2:11

Read the remarkable story in Mark 2:1-12 of the man who had been immobile for some time and was healed by the words and compassion of Jesus.

Pray that Jesus will heal any of your physical or spiritual ailments, according to His will and mercy.

33.

Does the Preacher Need to be Saved?

Shannon, our youngest son, has always had a mischievous streak and a great sense of humor. To this day, we don't know if the following situation was a result of one of his practical jokes or if he was getting back at his daddy for some punishment.

As soon as we moved to Fort Worth, Texas, so that my husband could attend seminary, we began visiting local churches in search of a church home. One Monday morning after one such visit, there was a knock at the door. Since he had no classes on Monday, my husband happened to be home alone. He invited in the two little ladies who stood there with Bibles in hand. One was a retired missionary. They quickly got to their purpose. "Your eight-year-old son filled out a visitor's card Sunday and on it indicated that his father was lost and needed a witness."

Steve assured the ladies that he was not only

a Christian, but that he was also a student at the seminary studying to become a minister. They were not to be deterred. They continued presenting to him the plan of salvation and encouraged him to repent and accept Christ.

The ladies were doing their part to carry out Christ's commission to go into the entire world and preach the gospel. I'm not really sure that he ever convinced the ladies that he was already a Christian. He did commend the ladies for their zeal and thanked them for the visit. Needless to say though, we chose not to join that church.

It is not good to have zeal without knowledge, nor to be hasty and miss the way. Proverbs 19:2

Read Colossians 4:2-6 for instructions on how to pray for doors to be opened for God's message to be delivered to the lost.

Ask God to direct you to someone today who needs His salvation and for the right words to say to them.

34.

Guilty, Guilty, Guilty!

Tyler, our youngest grandchild, brings a smile to the face of everyone who meets him. This three-year-old has the most beautiful, red, curly hair and a mischievous smile that would melt ice, along with the personality to match. As are most three-year-olds, he is quite active. He loves to climb, jump, and run.

In his classroom at church, there is a low window with a wide ledge from which the children like to jump. One Sunday he was involved in this caper when he fell and skinned his knee. His father had already scolded him for being rambunctious in the nursery before. This time he gave him strict instructions to not stand in the window and jump anymore. (Shannon is a good father who follows through to see that his children obey.)

One Wednesday night, Shannon was working, so Donna, his wife, took the children to church. When prayer meeting was over, she went to the nursery to get Tyler. The nursery worker told her that he had had an accident. It turned out that he had jumped from a doll bed, had fallen, and had burst his lip open.

After she dried his tears and took him home, Shannon called from work. Tyler always wanted to talk to his dad on the phone. Donna told him to tell Daddy what had happened to him, which he did.

Shannon was patiently trying to explain that jumping from the doll bed was just like jumping from the window ledge and that he shouldn't stand in the doll bed and jump anymore. Trying to draw the parallel, he said, "Tyler, you remember when I told you not to jump from the window ledge?"

Immediately, Tyler answered with an apology. "I'm sorry daddy. I won't jump from the window anymore."

With surprise Shannon asked, "Have you been jumping from the window again?"

"I'm sorry, Daddy. Here's Mommy. Talk to Mommy."

Guilty! Tyler was quick to get off the phone because he thought his father knew he had been disobedient.

Our Father *does* know our guilt, even before we confess, but he still expects us to confess our sins and to repent.

The price of sin is great, but forgiveness is available.

If we confess our sins, he is faithful and just and will forgive us our sins and purify us from all unrighteousness. I John 1:9

Read more about sin and the consequences of unconfesssed sin in I John 1:5-10.

Agree with God today about your sins, and ask for His forgiveness.

MUSIC MAKES
THE
HEART MERRY

*He put a new song in my mouth, a
hymn of praise to our God . . .*

Psalm 40:336.

35.

Let's Sing Hark the Herald

It was family vacation week at the beach. Steve and I, together with our sons' families, had rented a beach house, and we were having a great time. Because all of our sons live quite a distance from each other, the children love this special time to get together and play with their cousins.

Most nights we would grill out or cook at the beach house because it was easier than finding seating for that many people at a restaurant in a resort area. Despite this, we always made the effort to have at least one meal together at a nice restaurant. This night we were driving to a neighboring city to a famous steak house.

On our way to the restaurant, the children were entertaining themselves taking turns naming a song for the group to sing. Our granddaughters love music and have a great repertoire. However, Zack, our oldest grandson (who was about six at that time), spent most of his time outside playing ball and, therefore, was somewhat limited in his knowledge of song selections. As the girls would name a song, the group would sing it. When it came Zack's turn, he said, "Let's sing 'Hark the Herald Angels Sing.'" We did. The next time it came his turn, he, again, picked the same song just as though it was an original idea. This continued for about five rounds. The cousins complied joyfully while the adults doubled over with laughter after singing it the second time and then repeating it.

The Psalms repeatedly direct us to sing as an act of praise and worship. Joy seems to always be associated with singing.

My heart is steadfast, O God; I will sing and make music with all my soul. Psalm 108:1

Read the joyful chapter of Psalm 100.

Pray that God will always give you a song of praise in your heart.

36.

Count Your Blessings

Often there is a mixed message when the wrong hymn is chosen for a particular situation. Such was the case when my husband read his tearful resignation at one of his early pastorates. The young song leader already had planned the hymns for the service and gave no thought about changing them to fit the situation. Instead, just after my husband finished reading his letter of resignation, the song leader cheerfully said, "Now let's all sing 'Count Your Blessings.'" That might have hurt our feelings had we not known that he had not considered the implications; instead, we rejoiced in the meaningful words of the hymn.

God does instruct us to be thankful in all things. Thanking God for his abundant care and provision for us should come as natural to us as counting one, two, three.

. . . always giving thanks to God the Father

for everything, in the name of our Lord Jesus Christ.
Ephesians 5:20

Read Ephesians 5:1-20.

Pray that God will give you a thankful heart in all situations, both good and bad, realizing that He sees the whole picture when we see only a part.

37.

Singing Money

We once had a deacon named Otis who was a prominent businessman in town. He also served as our church clerk; therefore, money was forever on his mind. One Sunday, in the absence of our minister of music, Otis was to lead the music during the worship service. He stood with his hymnal and announced, "Please turn to three dollars and ninety-eight cents."

We all sang with merriment in our hearts that day, as we should always. More valuable than gold is the praise of God's children. Gold and silver are fickle and temporary; our desire to praise God should forever be with us.

Worship the Lord with gladness; come before him with joyful songs. Psalm 100:2

Read James 5:13-20.

Pray that God will give you a new song in your heart and the desire to continually praise Him in song.

38.

Round Young Virgin

Children often sing songs long before the meaning of the song hits home with them. As I child, I always sang Christmas carols with much vim and vigor. To the top of my lungs I would sing "—*Round young virgin* so tender and mild." I was a preteen before I checked out the words in a hymnal and realized that I should have been singing "round *yon* virgin."

Mary faced enough ridicule and embarrassment without my adding pounds to her. In the beginning, even Joseph doubted her story. Thankfully though, God sent an angel to him to confirm Mary's story. What God asked of Mary was no small task, but he provided for her needs, and she praised God for choosing her to be the mother of Jesus. May we all be as willing to do what God asks of us, just as Mary was.

You will be with child and give birth to a son, and you are to give him the name Jesus. Luke 1:31
Read Luke 1:26-35.

Pray that God will give you a willing heart to be what He wants you to be in His story.

39.

John's Own Son

When I was a child, my mother and father would often take my sisters and me to gospel singings to hear the John Daniel Quartet. John Daniel was Mother's first cousin. He convinced me that I was a really good singer because he would call me to the stage to sing with him on one particular song every time. It wasn't until I was much older that I realized why.

The song that I helped the quartet with was "That Meeting in the Air." There is a phrase in the song that says, "God's own Son will be leading one at that meeting in the air." Each time they got to that phrase, John would put the microphone to my mouth so the congregation would hear me sing loudly, "John's own son will be the leading one at that meeting in the air." Well, that was what the words sounded like to me.

The fact that Jesus is God's own Son is the message we should share with everyone we meet. Although earthly sons are important to us, let us not forget that if God had not been so generous to a lost, evil world by sacrificing His only begotten Son, we would have no hope and would exist in a world of total spiritual darkness.

No one who denies the Son has the Father; whoever acknowledges the Son has the Father also. I John 2:23

Read more about "sonship" in John 1:6-18.

Thank God today for sending His only begotten Son so that you may have eternal life.

40.

That Almost Wasn't in My Book

My mother, even into her nineties, was the pianist in her small country church, where she was much loved and appreciated. She had played there since she was thirteen years old. Even though she still played well and was very faithful to her job, her short-term memory was just about gone.

One Sunday the music director announced the page number of the hymn. Mother searched through the hymnal in one direction and then back the other way. This was repeated several times. Everyone there was feeling embarrassment for her. Finally she found the page. With a pleased smile she adjusted her book, looked up at the director, and said, "That song almost wasn't in my book." This relaxed and lightened the mood, and the congregation enjoyed a good laugh.

Not only do we find ourselves searching out spiritual things, but the Bible teaches us that the Holy Spirit does as well. It is through the Holy Spirit that these deep truths from God can be understood and applied in our lives.

. . . but God has revealed it to us by his Spirit. I Corinthians 2:10

Read I Corinthians 2:6-16 to see what these deep things are.

Pray that the Spirit will help you as you search out the deep truths of God. Also pray that when He searches your heart, He will find it pure and holy.

41.

Is It a Man or a Woman?

For many years my mother and dad, along with some of dad's brothers and sisters, would be asked to provide the music for the funerals of some friends and relatives. For one particular funeral, the family of the deceased requested they sing "If I Could Hear My Mother Pray Again." Looking a bit puzzled, my dad questioned, "But I thought this was a man's funeral?" And so it was, but they sang it anyway. Maybe there is no accounting for some people's musical choices or maybe the man did want to hear his mother pray again, but it was too late.

Paul writes in Colossians 4:2 "Devote yourselves to prayer, being watchful and thankful." Many mothers throughout history have certainly continued praying with vigilance for their sons and daughters. In our society where evil is lurking at every turn, daily prayer for our children is more important than ever.

Read Proverbs 15:28-33.

Pray for those in your family who need intercession today.

42.

Breath from God

Our choir director was stressing the importance of breath control while we were working on a particular anthem during rehearsal one night. Being a bit exasperated at our failure to follow his direction, he said, "Choir, right here you MUST grab a big breast and hold it." He meant breath.

Needless to say, the choir left early that night without ever accomplishing what our director had in mind because we couldn't regain our composure.

Breath is precious because it is the first gift God gave man. Because of its necessity for life, we should thank God and praise Him with every breath we take. In that way, we can truly pray without ceasing as we are instructed to do in I Thessalonians 5:17.

Let everything that has breath praise the Lord. Psalm 150:6

Read Genesis 2:1-7.

Pray that you will never take for granted nor be ungrateful for those things which are necessary for life that God gives you so freely, such as the air you breathe.

43.

I Must Tell Jesus

The walls were paper-thin in our small, married-student apartments at Samford University, but there existed a steel-strong fellowship and bond among the occupants because we all shared a common goal. The men who lived in the apartments with their wives and children had surrendered their lives to the Lord's ministry. All the men were struggling to get an education while trying to support their families by working afternoons and nights. Our next-door neighbor was a very gregarious man who had a sales job. Some of the guys who worked at night would take a study break some afternoons and play basketball in the courtyard. Often times, our salesman neighbor would come out of his apartment dressed in a nice suit, headed off to sell, but the temptation to play with the guys would be too great for him. He would end up taking off his coat to shoot "just a few," and before long, he would be too dirty and too late to make his intended sales calls. Later that night, after his family argument (which would always ensue), we would hear our friend picking out on the piano the hymn he would go to for solace—"I Must Tell Jesus." Every time we would hear him singing that song, we would say, "Gene's in trouble again." We still visit with these families with whom we made so many memories. When the group gathers now, someone will always mention and laugh about Gene singing "I Must Tell Jesus."

How important it is that we follow Gene's example and take our troubles and cares to Jesus. The first verse of that song goes, "I must tell Jesus all of my troubles. I cannot bear these burdens alone. In my despair, he truly will help me. I must tell Jesus, Jesus alone." May we remember today that whatever trouble might beset us, we have a friend and counselor in Jesus, our Lord.

In the same way, the Spirit helps us in our weakness. We do not know what we ought to pray for, but the Spirit himself intercedes for us with groans that words cannot express. Romans 8:26

Continue reading in Romans 8:26-39.

Today, name your troubles to the Lord. Then be willing to allow the Spirit to intercede for you for God's will to be done.

44.

Where Could I Go?

We often sang that lively old hymn, "Where Could I Go?" in the little country church where I spent my childhood and teen years. We young people would sit near the rear of the church, hoping that our misbehavior would go unnoticed by our parents. Being less than reverent, we often took liberties with the words of the hymns. In this particular hymn we changed the words, "needing a friend to help me in the end" to "needing a friend to kick me in the end." Little did we realize at the time that that was what we truly needed—a friend to kick us in the end.

Friends should show love at all times. Friends celebrate when we do things right. When we need upbraiding, love needs to be tough. Love tells the truth to help a friend. Love throws a barrier in the path of a friend who is headed in the wrong direction. If you have a friend who is going the wrong direction, show him the right path through the love of the Lord.

A friend loves at all times, and a brother is born for adversity. Proverbs 17:17

Read about Jesus' concern for his friends in John 17:8-20.

Pray that you will be a friend to those around you showing both compassion and tough love when needed.

45.

Why Are They Singing So Loud?

My sister sang in her college's choir. One year she invited our family to attend their Christmas concert. As they sang a selection from "Messiah," the music built to a beautiful crescendo and then suddenly, there was a small rest. It was at that choice point that my young son screamed, "Mommy, why are they singing so loud?" The beautiful moment was interrupted by uproarious laughter from those around.

Does your heart sing loudly with daily praise to the Lord? We are told in the scriptures that if we don't praise the Lord, the rocks and hills will cry out. The Lord WILL be praised. Let's not wait for the rocks to do it.

Praise the Lord! How good it is to sing praises to our God, how pleasant and fitting to praise him! Psalm 147:1

Read the instructions from the Lord to sing praises in Psalms 149 and 150.

Praise the Lord for twenty specific things today as you pray.

Country Church Memories

I thank my God every time
I remember you.

Philippians 1:3

46.

God - Not a Respectable Person???

The small country church where I grew up holds many fond memories for me. Even though our pastors were often uneducated, they were men of God with good hearts and pure intentions. One of these pastors had difficulty reading; therefore, he mispronounced many words. One of his favorite Bible phrases was "God is no respecter of persons." The problem was he read and quoted the verse as, "God is not a respectable person."

He used the verse in the correct context and most of the regular attendees understood his meaning, but his words sent a confusing message to visitors and to those who were not accustomed to his regular language blunders.

We often find ourselves blundering when we try to communicate the sincere desires of our hearts to God. Isn't it nice to know that the Holy Spirit is there to intercede for us in our weakness? Thankfully, God knows the desires and intents of our hearts.

Delight yourself in the LORD and he will give you the desires of your heart. Psalm 37:4
Read Malachi chapter 1.
Pray that God will know your needs and intentions, even when you can't express them.

47.

A World Full of 'Genuine' Delinquents

(pronounced "gin' u in")

Our country preacher once tried to stress the importance of children obeying their parents. He was speaking of the disrespectful nature of many teens. He said, "Everywhere you look in our world today, you see them 'gin' u ine' delinquents." (He was referring to juvenile delinquents.)

Although we have some wonderful, committed Christian young people in our world today, some teens have never been taught to respect people who are in authority over them. It is important for children to live under the authority of their parents and, just as importantly, for parents to live holy lives that demand the respect of their children. Children's learning to respect parental authority is a precursor to their respecting and acknowledging God's divine authority in their lives.

Train a child in the way he should go, and

when he is old he will not turn from it. Proverbs 22:6

Read the following verses: Proverbs 23:13, Isaiah 9:7, Proverbs 31:28, and Matthew 10:12.

First, pray that parents will see the necessity of bringing up children in the fear and admonition of the Lord; and, second, pray that our nation's children will have Godly respect for those in authority over them.

48.

Brassieres in Church

In that same country church, not only was the pastor short on education and reading skills, but some of the members of the church were literacy-challenged as well.

One of our older saintly ladies was always willing to do all she could for Christ and His church. She attended and participated in every activity and program offered at the church. As was customary, she got up one Sunday night during the hour devoted to the training of church members in doctrine and missions (which was then called "Training Union") to read her "part" (a paragraph or two from the lesson for the night) from the Baptist quarterly publication. Her part was about the challenges of spreading the gospel in Brazil, but every time she came to the word Brazil, she would say "brassiere" instead. I'm not sure if she even understood the meaning of what she was reading, but she definitely was a willing worker with great zeal.

Thankfully, God is more concerned with our

availability and our obedience than He is with our ability or level of skill. Often times we make the excuse that others are more qualified than we are to do certain Christian tasks. While that may very well be true, there are plenty of times when God would rather have a person who is less qualified but more willing to do what He asks than to have someone who is highly qualified but doesn't have a servant's heart. How willing are you to say, "Lord, I'll do what you enable me to do"?

> . . . *The spirit is willing, but the body is weak.*
> *Matthew 26:41*

Read Matthew 5:13-20.

Pray for those who have more desire to do God's work than they have ability and that God will bless their efforts. Also pray that God will give you knowledge, wisdom, and the desire to spread His word.

49.

What's Good Enough for Peter and Paul

Often times we are afraid of the unknown. So it was with one of my Sunday School teachers in that same country church when I was a youth. The Phillip's translation of the Bible was just coming into vogue. Intending to encourage us to keep true to God's word, the teacher admonished us to avoid these new "man-made" translations. Very sincerely he said, "If the King James Version was good enough for Peter and Paul, it's good enough for me and should be good enough for you."

Though his factual information was in error, the teaching of the importance of keeping the scriptures pure was certainly on target. We are blessed by the years of work that many have given to provide translations which remain true to the Word and that put the scriptures in today's language.

I tell you the truth, until heaven and earth disappear, not the smallest letter, not the least stroke

of a pen, will by any means disappear from the Law until everything is accomplished. Matthew 5:18
Read Luke 4:21-27.

Pray that the true word of God will be preserved and hidden in your heart so that you may see God and so that you will always be willing and eager to share it with others.

50.

Perfection is Hard to Come By

Memories of happy and funny times in that little country church continue to flood my mind. Another of our pastors was once preaching about the sinful nature of man and the perfection of Jesus. My dad worked long hours in our country store and service station and rarely had a chance to sit quietly. When he did, he would inevitably fall asleep, as was the case one particular Sunday morning as he sat listening to a sermon.

The preacher came to a crucial part of his sermon and for emphasis rhetorically asked, "If there is a perfect man in the house, would he just now raise his hand?" My dad in his daze only heard "raise your hand" and thought that we were voting on something. He gradually slipped his hand high for all to see. When one of my aunts (who always saw humor in life) saw him raise his hand, she could not contain her laughter. When she broke the reverent silence, the others who also saw him also enjoyed a good laugh at his expense.

The pastor later jokingly said, "You thought Hugh was asleep, but he wasn't. Maybe he does think he's perfect."

No, there is not one on this Earth who can truthfully boast of perfection. Because of mankind's sinful nature, we can only be made clean and acceptable to our Heavenly Father through accepting His perfect sacrifice—Jesus Christ—for our sins.

. . . *for all have sinned and fall short of the glory of God. Romans 3:23*

Read Matthew 5:21-48.

Thank God that even as you were a sinner, He sent His perfect son that you might have life and have it more abundantly.

51.

Would the Mothers Please Stand?

Old age brings with it some unpleasant side effects. We once had a man in our congregation who suffered from many of them. For one thing, his driving skills had badly deteriorated. He seemed to always forget to look when he backed out onto the busy highway to come to church. Fortunately, since ours was a small community, our congregation knew each other well, where each member lived, and the comings and goings of most. Therefore, the congregation and God knew when he would be backing out of his drive to come to church, so all watched out for him.

Another problem that arose was caused by this gentleman's inability to hear well. In order that he might understand more of the service, he always sat on the first pew directly in front of the preacher. Every Mother's Day, the pastor would recognize the mothers in the congregation by having them stand. Since my mother was the pianist, she also sat on that front pew. On one particular Mother's Day, taking his cue from my mother, Uncle Elrod (as this man was known in the community) stood with the mothers when she stood. To a group of young people who always sat much farther back (and I was among them), this was hilarious.

It seems that young people forget that with each passing year, they grow closer to some of these problems themselves. God admonishes us to respect and care for our old people. He also showed His love for the young. We should remember the Golden Rule in dealing with others—"Do unto others as you would have them do unto you."

I was young and now I am old, yet I have never seen the righteous forsaken or their children begging bread. Psalm 37:25

Read Psalm 37:23-26.

Pray that you will remember your Creator in the days of your youth, as well as in your old age.

52.

Oh, God, That's Too Much Salt

An employee who worked at my mom and dad's restaurant attended a country church in a very remote mountain area. She once told the story of a mountain man from her church who was in his forties before he came to the Lord. He had lived a really rough life filled with drinking, cursing, and fighting. Therefore he didn't know "church-ese" as those of us who have attended church all of our lives do. What he did know was to take his burdens and cares to the Lord in prayer. One Sunday when the preacher called on him to pray, he prayed like this:

Dear Lord, you know times have been tough lately. Since I quit bootlegging, I don't have the money I need to feed my family. If you can help us, Lord, we need a barrel of flour. Lord, we need a barrel of sugar. Father, we need some pepper and a barrel of salt—Oh, d____, we don't need that much salt, God.

Even though the Lord still had some work to

do in him, the man did have the faith to ask God for his daily needs.

Yes, God is our Lord; He is our Father, and just as our earthly fathers sometimes know our needs before we ask, they still like for us to communicate them. God is omnipotent; he knows better than we do what we need. Still, we do need to ask. By doing so, we acknowledge Him as our provider. Jesus, himself, taught us to pray.

Give us today our daily bread. Matthew 6:11

Read Jesus' discourse on prayer in Matthew 6:1-14.

Through prayer, today, acknowledge God as your provider. Tell Him your needs, both great and small. He cares and answers them all.

53.

How Fast Did He Have to Run?

We had an unusually large youth group at that country church where I grew up. On Sunday nights during the "Training Union" hour we often had Bible drills. We always had to deliver our assigned "parts" from our quarterly from memory—good training that I've never forgotten. We played together, prayed together, and joked together (sometimes a bit inappropriately).

We always felt a freedom to ask for prayer for any need or concern we might have had. During one of our serious prayer sessions, one of the young men requested prayer for his father. "What's wrong with your dad?" questioned our leader.

"I don't know, but he's passing blood."

One of our young men looked a bit like Red Buttons, a well-known, red-headed, freckle-faced comedian from the sixties, and possessed a similar sense of humor. This time he was somewhat irreverent when he blurted out, "How fast did he have to run to pass it?" Needless to say, his humor wasn't graciously received that night.

It was there, in that youth "Training Union" class, where we learned to pray in faith.

Is any one of you in trouble? He should pray. Is anyone happy? Let him sing songs of praise. Is any one of you sick? He should call the elders of the church to pray over him and anoint him with oil in the name of the Lord. James 5:13-14

Read all of James 5 to discover how to react to hardships.

Today, pray for those you know who need the healing hand of Jesus and for those who are troubled with life's problems.

Baptize Them in the Name of the Lord

And whatever you do, whether in word or deed, do it all in the name of the Lord Jesus, giving thanks to God the Father through him.

Colossians 3:17

54.

Something I've Always Wanted to Do

As a child, I had a pastor who was a very "persistent" evangelist. We had a man in our community who was very hardened against the idea of becoming a Christian and even more hardened against evangelistic efforts.

With the help of the Holy Spirit, the two men met. The pastor went to his house and stayed with the rapscallion until he wore the sinner down and convinced him to surrender his life to Jesus.

The occasion on which this man was baptized was a great event in our church. That Sunday the church was filled to capacity with people who were anticipating this wonderful event. Many of them had previously attempted to witness to him and had prayed for him relentlessly.

With much emotion, the pastor entered the baptistery with the man and said, "Crowley, this is something I've wanted to do for a long time." With those words, he zealously took Crowley back and accidentally whacked his head on the wall of the baptistery.

There was no doubt in anyone's mind that day about the genuineness of Crowley's salvation. Before his conversion, he would have cursed out the preacher at best, and at worst, would have killed him for such an action. Instead, he just rubbed the knot on his head and smiled.

This gave a whole new meaning to the verse, *"Therefore, if anyone is in Christ, he is a new creation; the old has gone, the new has come!" II Corinthians 5:17*

Read Romans 10:1-15.

Pray for God to soften the hearts which have hardened toward Him. Pray for the salvation of those on your top ten "Most Wanted for Christ" list.

55.

A Sunday Swim

A friend of ours tells of the time when things were ready for a baptismal service at his church. The candidates were prepared and waiting; the pastor was giving them last-minute instructions; the congregation sat in quiet reverence. Suddenly a young boy was tempted a little too strongly by the clear pool of water. He jumped in for a swim across the baptistery as the entire congregation looked on in shock.

Perhaps he had heard the story of Naaman being told to dip seven times in the Jordan River to be healed. He may have thought that if seven dips would do a body good that a swim would do it even better. It is our sacred duty to obey God in following Jesus in baptism.

And now what are you waiting for? Get up, be baptized and wash your sins away, calling on his name. Acts 22:16

Read the story of Naaman's strange instructions from the Lord in II Kings 5.

Pray that in faith, you will be able to follow

God's instructions, regardless of how large or small the task seems to be.

56.

Baptize Him; Don't Drown Him

As is the ordinary custom in most Methodist churches, when a person is baptized, he or she is sprinkled with water rather than being immersed in it. This was the standard procedure followed by one Methodist pastor friend in Birmingham, Alabama. One time, however, this pastor friend of ours had a man to join his congregation who asked for baptism by immersion. So the Methodist pastor asked a Baptist pastor friend if he might use the baptistery in his church one Sunday afternoon. The pastor gladly agreed. He said, "Jim, the church custodian, will lay out the robes and waders for you and will be here if you need any assistance."

The Methodist pastor thanked him graciously, and each man went on his way. On Monday morning, the Baptist pastor asked Jim (the church custodian) how the baptizing had gone. He replied, "Bro. John, you just ain't goin' to believe this. That preacher put them waders on the man he was about to baptize instead of wearing them himself. When he took him back into the waters, them waders filled up with water, and I had to jump in there with him to get that man out before he drowned."

If the man had it to do over, he might not have been as eager to be immersed, as was the eunuch that asked to be baptized by Phillip. Reflect today on the symbolism of baptism. We are buried as was Christ. Just as Christ arose from the dead, we arise as a new creature in Christ.

As they traveled along the road, they came to some water and the eunuch said, "Look, here is water. Why shouldn't I be baptized?" Acts 8:36

Read Acts 8:26-40.

Pray that men everywhere will be eager to read the word of God and, in so doing, will be convicted of their sins. Also pray that they, in turn will seek baptism by water as well as baptism in the Holy Ghost.

57.

Repeat after Me

An evangelist friend of ours tells the story of a young lady who once followed his instructions too closely during her baptism. When he was a young pastor, his mind often worked faster than his mouth, which caused a speech impediment.

In one of his first baptismal services, he was to baptize a lady named Marvalene Wainwright. However, in his nervousness and haste, he told her to repeat after him, "I, Mavaween Wainwight . . ."

She did exactly as he instructed; she repeated, "I, Mavaween Wainwight . . ."

We as humans may often make mistakes in calling people's names, but our Heavenly Father knows her name and ours. Names are important to God in many ways. Read the scripture verses today and realize that there is no sweeter name than "Christian" for us to be called.

A good name is more desirable than great riches; to be esteemed is better than silver or gold. Proverbs 22:1

Read more of what the Bible says about names in Psalm 8:1, Psalm 72:17, Psalm 102:15, and John 15:16.

Pray that your life will be lived in such a manner that the name "Christian" will fit you appropriately.

Right Meaning; Wrong Word

For the ear tests words as the tongue tastes food.

Job 34:3

(Malapropism -the usually unintentional humorous misuse or distortion of a word or phrase.)

58.

A Gift of Hospitalization

I have a dear friend who is simply a fountain of malapropisms. She is a sweet, dedicated Christian who has the purest of intentions. Once, she was leading a group in the FAITH ministry, and her daughter-in-law was in the group. A young woman, whom they visited, had graciously invited them in and had allowed them to share the plan of salvation with her. Upon leaving, my friend instructed her daughter-in-law in proper etiquette. She said, "Kayra, you need to sit down when you get home and write this lady a note, thanking her for her *hospitalization*."

Thankfully, Kayra had known her mother-in-law long enough to understand that she was referring to the lady's *hospitality*.

Much is said in the Bible about offering hospitality. My favorite of these passages is Hebrews 13. Read this chapter noting verse 2, *"Do not forget to entertain strangers, for by so doing some people have entertained angels without knowing it."*

Pray that God will open your eyes and heart to the possibilities of entertaining angels by making you willing to open your home to people in the name of Christ.

59.

Go Tell It Everywhere

Our church choir's pseudo-operatic soprano (every church has one), who always sang louder and longer than everybody else, reminded us during a Wednesday night choir rehearsal that the message of the Lord should not be limited by geographical boundaries nor by song lyrics.

As we were practicing "Ye Shall Be Witnesses" and came to the section that says, "Jerusalem, Judea, Samaria, and unto the ends of the world," again, louder and longer than anyone else, "Mrs. Opera" sang, "Je-ru-sa-lem, Judea, Ko-re-a . . ."

Although she got her words confused, her message was sound. We are to be witnesses throughout the world. How big is your world (or scope of witness)? With whom have you shared the good news of Jesus Christ? Ask God for an opportunity today to share the gospel.

Therefore go and make disciples of all nations, baptizing them in the name of the Father and of the Son and of the Holy Spirit. Matthew 28:19

Humorous Happenings in Holy Places

Read Matthew 28:16-20.

Pray that God will reveal to you just where and how He wants you to spread His word and that He will give you the courage and ability to do so.

60.

Gold, Frankenstein, and Myrrh

Years ago, my mom took on the task of directing the church's Christmas play. Twin boys, who had little experience in church, had started attending. When she cast the play, one of the twins showed up to try out for a part. Since the congregation was small, she knew she needed all of the warm bodies that were willing, so she cast the boy as a wise man.

At every practice, she felt that she had to start over with that child because he couldn't remember what to do. Finally, she realized that one twin was showing up one time, and the other, the next. She admonished them that the same one needed to come each time. She told the other one that he could have a non-speaking part.

On the night of the performance, the twin, who elected to do the speaking part, took to heart Mom's instructions about speaking loudly. He shouted, "We wise men bring to Jesus, gold, 'frankenstein,' and myrrh.

Although the play was not intended as a comedy, it certainly brought the house down with laughter that night. What gift have you brought to Jesus? He wants nothing less than your all.

On coming to the house, they saw the child with his mother Mary, and they bowed down and worshiped him. Then they opened their treasures and presented him with gifts of gold and of incense and of myrrh. Matthew 2:11

Read the story of the wise men in Matthew 2.

Pray that your heart will be made eager to present the very best gifts you have to Christ.

61.

None Made the Honor Choir

One year, the kids in our children's choir had diligently practiced to land a spot in the County Honor Competition Choir. When the time came to announce the names of the ones who had been selected for it, the weekly church mail-out newsletter reported in the "Praise Items," "**None** of our children made the honor choir and will be going to Gadsden to compete." Actually, it should have said, "**Nine** of our children . . ." A staff member from a neighboring church called our minister of music and questioned why he would celebrate the children's failure.

Very few situations in life call for celebration over losing something, but there are many Biblical principles which are juxtaposed to society's standards. In one story, two women had a dispute, each claiming that a baby belonged to her. In order to settle the argument, King Solomon ordered his servants to cut the child in two and to give half the baby to one woman and half of the baby to the other. The real mother said, "No! Please give her the baby! Don't kill him!" Solomon then ruled that the baby be given to her for her desire to see the baby live over keeping him for herself proved that she was the legitimate mother. In another story, Abraham was willing to sacrifice his son in order to obey God; then, at the last moment, God provided a scapegoat. When we completely surrender our lives to Christ, we win the greatest prize—salvation.

For whoever wants to save his life will lose it, but whoever loses his life for me will find it. Matthew 16:25

Read Matthew 16:24-27 for a Biblical principle that seems to contradict what society teaches.

Pray that the Father will make you aware of the importance of sacrificing your own life and your own will in exchange for eternal salvation.

62.

A Confis'ticated (rhymes with sophisticated) Church

My dad is a great joker. It is a rare occasion that he can stay completely serious about anything. It was one of those rare occasions when we were having a solemn conversation. We were discussing how different churches are in their worship styles. He commented that it took all kinds of churches to appeal to the different tastes of people. He said, "For example your church is a lot more 'confisticated' than ours."

My mother, who is known for creating words to suit her own purposes, replied, "Oh, Hugh, it's not 'confisticated'; it's 'sophisticated.'"

Puzzled, he asked, "Well, what does 'confisticated' mean then?"

With all sincerity she replied, "Ah, you know, it's like when the sheriff goes out and 'confis'ticates' the bootleggers' whiskey."

Churches do worship in many different ways; some use high church music accompanied with beautiful pipe organs, while others sing only contemporary songs played by bands. Some follow a liturgy; others have a very casual order of service. The method is not the main issue of concern, but the object and intentions of the heart are. God is never honored by empty rituals, but instead honors true praise.

Through Jesus, therefore, let us continually offer to God a sacrifice of praise—the fruit of lips that confess his name. Hebrews 13:15

Read Hebrews 13:7-25 to see some things of worship that honor God.

Pray that your praise and sacrifice will be unadulterated and will be an acceptable offering of worship unto the Lord.

63.

Drinking from the Coffee Urinal

The superintendent of one of our adult Sunday School departments, who was also an engineer at a plant which made bathroom fixtures, made a startling announcement one Sunday morning. He announced, "Everyone, come thirty minutes early next Sunday morning for a time of food and fellowship. We will have doughnuts and a big urinal (meaning urn) of coffee."

Not many wanted coffee from that kind of vessel. Neither does God want prayers and praise from unclean vessels. Our first petition when coming to His throne in prayer should be a prayer of confession and repentance, asking God to cleanse us from all unrighteousness. Only through an act of God can sinful man be pure enough to offer acceptable worship and praise to a Holy God. We are God's vessels.

But the Lord said to Ananias, "Go! This man is my chosen instrument [vessel] to carry my name before the Gentiles and their kings and before the people of Israel." Acts 9:15

Read I Thessalonians 4:1-12.

Pray that God will cleanse you and make you a clean vessel to serve Him.

64.

A Gift Both From God and To God

A young mother was once trying to help my husband remember a special day in her life. She said, "You remember the day you circumcised our daughter, Gina?" His shocked expression made her rethink her words. Actually, she was referring to the day he "dedicated" her daughter which was a very special day. A child dedication service is a time when parents acknowledge that their child is a gift from God, and that only **HE** holds the master plan for the child's optimum happiness. Therefore, they give the child back to God, in faith, believing that He will care for and guide the child's path in life.

Regardless of the word the mother used, it is of utmost importance that parents remember that God lets us have children to see what we will do as parents. Wise parents recognize that their wisdom is insufficient for making the best decisions concerning their child and that it is of greatest importance for them to give their child over to Him.

Luke 2:22 gives the account of Mary and

Joseph's presenting Jesus to the Lord. It says, *"When the time of their purification according to the Law of Moses had been completed, Joseph and Mary took him to Jerusalem to present him to the Lord."*

Read the entire account of this dedication event in Luke 2:21-40.

Pray that God will give you the wisdom to recognize your weaknesses and His superior strength and that you will entrust your greatest possessions, your children, to Him who loves them even more than you do.

My Funny Husband and other Funny Things

The boundary lines have fallen for me in pleasant places; surely I have a delightful inheritance.

Psalm 16:6

A Visitor?

65.

An Unwelcome Visitor at Church

As my husband was making announcements one Sunday morning, a huge horsefly made its way into church and up to the pulpit. It flew around his head, then through the choir loft where I was sitting, back to his head, back to the choir loft, and on and on. For fear that this would continue to disrupt worship, or even worse, fly into his mouth when he began preaching, I took it upon myself to remedy the situation.

On the next pass the fly made through the choir, I was poised and ready. I cupped my hand and intended to snatch the fly out of the air to end the disturbance. Instead, I created an even greater one. Instead of snatching the fly, I accidentally caught my glasses with my finger on that quick swing. They slung off, hit the lady next to me, and then ricocheted to the back row of the choir. The lady next to me thought I had slapped her, and she turned around in surprise and disgust, only to discover the shocked look on my face. The men on the back row were puzzled, trying to figure out where the glasses came from. Worship was definitely disrupted that Sunday.

Although the devil will use any means, even a fly, to keep people from doing it, worshiping God is a privilege; it is also a command from God which we must not ignore. Bowing before God shows our submission to the King of Kings. There is an old saying, "Man is never taller than when he in on his knees before God."

Come, let us bow down in worship, let us kneel before the Lord our Maker. Psalm 95:6

Read Psalms 95 and 96.

Pray that God will find your worship and praise to be acceptable gifts that you lay before Him. Praise Him for who He is, for what He has done, and for what He will do.

66.

A State of Contentment

My husband has never faired well in hot weather. Making a holy pilgrimage to the seminary in Fort Worth, Texas, didn't change that one bit. For the years we lived there, seldom did a day pass without his grumbling about the weather. Having had about enough of his complaints, I thought I would end them with scripture. I told him, "Paul taught us to be content whatever state we are in."

For that, he had a quick comeback. "That just proves one thing; Paul never lived in Texas."

Although we had a laugh at his comeback, we both now realize the importance of being content regardless of our circumstances. We acknowledge that Christ is sufficient in every situation, even in the Texas heat.

A few years earlier I had received a peace and understanding about this principle. We had been financially strapped while we were in college. Some days my desire for material things outweighed my pocketbook. I prayed that God would take from me the desire for the things I didn't really need and provide me and mine with the things that we did. He did that very thing.

But godliness with contentment is great gain.
I Timothy 6:6

Read Philippians 4:10-23.

Pray that God will teach you the art of contentment, regardless of your circumstances.

67.

They'll Think I've Gone to Hell

A bi-vocational minister in our area worked at the hospital in the transportation department. Once, when he was transporting a ninety-three-year-old woman to X-ray, he struck up a conversation with her. She told him that she was the youngest of thirteen children and that she was the only one living. She looked up at him very seriously and said, "If I don't hurry up and die, the rest of my family is going to think I went to Hell."

Although this woman was making a joke *about* Hell, some people think Hell *is* a joke. The Bible teaches differently. If we choose to take Christ as our Savior, we have the assurance of Heaven as our final destination; if we don't, there is a Hell awaiting us.

Revelation 20:15 says, "If anyone's name was not found written in the book of life, he was thrown into the lake of fire."

He will punish those who do not know God and do not obey the gospel of our Lord Jesus. They will be punished with everlasting destruction and shut out from the presence of the Lord and from the majesty of his power. II Thessalonians 1:8-9

Read Revelation 21:3-27 to find the reward awaiting those who trust Him.

Pray for at least three people today who do not have the assurance of salvation and a home in heaven.

68.

Beautiful Feet

In his first pastorate, my husband was working diligently to improve his preaching with every sermon. When we would get in the car after the service and before we would even get out of the churchyard, he would look to me for a critique of his sermon. Usually I gave him a very favorable one.

One Sunday he seemed to lose his place and to forget what point he was trying to make in his sermon. His text was Romans 10:15 *"How beautiful are the feet of those who bring good news!"* At first he quoted the verse. Then he quoted it again emphasizing a different word: "How beautiful are the FEET of those . . ." and then, "How BEAUTIFUL are the feet of those . . ." and then, "How beautiful are the feet of THOSE . . ." He continued in this manner until he had emphasized, individually, just about every word in the verse and had found his train of thought again.

When he turned to me that particular Sunday for comments, all I could say was, "Well, all I got from the sermon today was that you have beautiful feet."

The feet are used in many scriptures to represent the whole:

Psalm 8:6 says, *"You made him ruler over the works of your hands; you put everything under his feet:"* In Zechariah 14:4, Zechariah prophesied, " . . . *His feet will stand on the Mount of Olives . . ."* Matthew 28:8-9 says, *"So the women hurried away from the tomb, afraid yet filled with joy, and ran to tell his disciples. Suddenly Jesus met them. 'Greetings,' he said. They came to him, clasped his feet and worshiped him."* In John 13:6-8, Jesus washed Peter's feet in a demonstration of service. Other references to the feet of Jesus are as follows: Luke 8:35, 41; Luke 17:16; John 11:32; John 12:3; and Revelation 19:10.

Read Romans 10 in its entirety to see the significance of beautiful feet.

Pray that your feet will make many worthwhile steps to spread the gospel of peace to others.

69.

The Time Has Come

We once had an elderly man who was almost deaf in one of our congregations. For Christmas, his children had given him a watch with an alarm on it to help him remember when to take his medications. It was set to go off at twelve noon each day. The only problem was he couldn't hear it, but everyone else could.

Well, anytime the Sunday service went a little long, everyone was reminded because the watch beeped incessantly. If people came down for prayer, they knew to make it fast for the watch's alarm was about to sound. If people joined the church, the announcement of their names and decisions could not be heard because the annoying watch sounded louder.

Although we may not have an audible alarm to warn us that the time for His return is drawing nigh, God's word definitely warns us to "be ready in season and out of season" (see II Timothy 4:2).

With the arrival of a new millennium, some

predicted gloom and doom; some were panicky because of the unknown. As Christians, our comfort and warning come from God's word. The following verse reminds us that all of time—past, present, and future—are in His hands:

No one knows about that day or hour, not even the angels in heaven, nor the Son, but only the Father. Matthew 24:36

Read Matthew 24:32-51.

Pray that God will help you in your daily activity to be ready for whatever He has in store for you and that you will truly be ready for His return in every season.

70.

Spell It, Please

My husband, who is usually really good at remembering names, had a memory lapse one Sunday as he was about to introduce a new member to the congregation. He had visited the man and his family on numerous occasions to encourage them to join our church, but for some unknown reason, he drew a blank when he tried to say the man's name. Thinking he could cover without the man being any wiser to his forgetfulness, he asked him, "Now how is it that you spell your name?"

The man replied with a knowing grin on his face, "J-O-E S-M-I-T-H."

We all have times of forgetfulness, but it is most important that we remember some essentials: We must remember whose we are and who created us from dust. We must remember the laws of God. We must remember how fleeting life is.

Remember your Creator in the days of your youth . . . Ecclesiastes 12:1

Remember the Sabbath day by keeping it holy. Exodus 20:8

Remember . . . that my life is but a breath . . . Job 7:7

Read Jeremiah 31:27-40 (paying special attention to verse 34) to discover what the Lord promises He will remember no more.

Pray that your mind will be sharp and alert to remember the promises and covenant of the Lord.

71.

Is the Church Going to the Dogs?

In earlier days the parsonage or manse was always next to the church. We lived in one such house when our boys were young. One of our church members thought that these three boys really needed a dog. Since this member's dog had just had a litter of puppies, he eagerly gave the boys one. This puppy was truly blessed by God because he seemed to come through many trials and troubles, sunny side up. For example, one year I raked out all the Thanksgiving table scraps, not knowing that a puppy had no stopping sense about eating. Later, I looked out the window and saw the puppy with his belly dragging the ground. On another occasion, one of my sons was practicing his casting skills in the yard and caught the dog in the ear. The hook had to be surgically removed. Following the surgery, the boys' entertainment of the day was to try to get the dog to walk after he had been sedated. He would stagger and stumble all over the yard.

Ultimately, all of these mishaps just seemed

to make the dog love the family more and the family love him more. He followed us everywhere. Most Sundays he greeted us, as well as all the well-dressed church ladies, by jumping on us as we came out of church. We finally resorted to locking him under the house before we went to church. Inevitably, he would break free and would be there to greet all with his tail wagging and his paws on the ladies' dresses. Most of the parishioners took this in stride or bore it in silence until one dreadful day.

The boys had gone out to the church one weekday to ask their dad something. They didn't realize the dog followed them in, but later, everyone else knew he had. The dog, apparently, had musical aspirations because he got in the choir loft and demolished all the hymnals. When some of the members came in, they were met by piles of pages from the hymnals all over the sanctuary.

If only we could all be as eager and happy to go to the Lord's house as the dog seemed to be! Throughout the Bible we are taught the value of assembling ourselves together to worship the Lord. There is multiplied spiritual strength when Christians join in worship. Bonds of friendship are formed when people praise God together. Solace is found in assembling ourselves before God.

I rejoiced with those who said to me, "Let us go to the house of the LORD." Psalm 122:1

Read all of Psalm 122.

Pray that you will truly count it a joy and privilege to gather with other Christians in the house of the Lord to worship. Thank God for this opportunity that we take so lightly when others around the world have to meet secretly to worship.

72.

Woe is Me for I am Undone

One of my uncles continued making the effort to go to church even after he had gotten old and feeble and had to be helped with almost everything. I guess my grandfather had instilled in all of his twelve children the importance of going to church to worship so strongly that this uncle just couldn't stay home, even if it were the easier thing to do. He had long since given up the practice of dressing up in a suit and tie, however. His daily attire of overalls just seemed the easiest thing to wear. Everyone understood and just admired his efforts to make it to church.

One Sunday morning, his daughter was helping her father to his usual seat near the front of the church when the galluses on his too-big overalls came loose and his pants hit the floor. She quickly came to his rescue and pulled them up and fastened them for him. Undaunted, he just continued to his seat. I guess he felt a kinship to Isaiah who said in Isaiah 6:5, *"Woe is me for I am undone."(NKJV)*

When Isaiah approached God, he realized

how unworthy he was. In the same way, when we draw near to God, we realize our shortcomings and insufficiencies as we stand in awe of His righteousness and completeness.

*Then I said: "O LORD, God of heaven, the great and **awesome** God, who keeps his covenant of love with those who love him and obey his commands ..." Nehemiah 1:5*

Isaiah 6 gives the order in which we should examine ourselves and others. First, we must look to a Holy God, second, we must acknowledge our own sins, and third, after we have looked to God and then inwardly to ourselves, we may view others in that perspective. When Isaiah looked up and saw the holiness of God, he was then moved to examine his own heart and life. Only then was it appropriate for him to look outward to the sins of others.

Look up and praise God for who He is; then look inward to discover your sins. Once you have discovered your sins, confess them, and finally accept God's forgiveness for them.

73.

Santa and the Firecrackers

When my husband was a child, it was the custom in his church for Santa to make an appearance one Sunday night before Christmas to give all of the children gifts. The Santa who was employed for this occasion, shall we say, got into the 'Christmas spirits' a little early. He was extremely jolly with the children, but, for awhile, the parents didn't know that he was actually drunk. During a deacon's long prayer, *Santa* thought he would liven up things a bit and took some firecrackers from his pocket and started shooting them in church. The deacons saw to it that Santa made an early departure.

Even though the event still provides some laughs today, the seriousness of what alcohol does to people cannot be laughed at. Alcohol is one of the most common causes for deaths. Often it is a precursor to drug use for some people who have addictive tendencies. It is also responsible for many problems—family, financial, physical, emotional, and spiritual. The abuse of alcohol hampers the witness of many Christians. The Bible speaks strongly against drunkenness.

The acts of the sinful nature are obvious: sexual immorality, impurity and debauchery; idolatry and witchcraft; hatred, discord, jealousy, fits of rage, selfish ambition, dissensions, factions and envy; **drunkenness,** *orgies, and the like. I warn you, as I did before, that those who live like this will not inherit the kingdom of God. Galatians 5:19-21*

Read Proverbs 20:1, Ephesians 5:8, and Romans 13:13.

Pray for families you know who are presently suffering due to alcohol. Ask God to help you to keep your body holy because you are the temple of God.

74.

Split Britches

It was the Wednesday night before Thanksgiving. As was customary for this particular pre-holiday service, the Methodist and Baptist churches came together for a special Thanksgiving service. This one was very special. My husband had just been called to the church as associate pastor. He and I were both attending college at the time, and we had three children. The community thought it would be an appropriate time to give the new preacher a "pounding." (I believe this event originally got its name from people bringing a pound of something—sugar, coffee, flour, etc.) In the generous spirit of the season, the churches went overboard in their giving. After my husband preached a moving Thanksgiving sermon, we were presented the many boxes of food. My husband picked up a box, as did many of the other men, to take it to our car. People were standing around fellowshipping, and many wanted to get to know the new preacher and his family.

After awhile, one of our sons came to me and

said, "Daddy said for me to come get you." I noticed my husband was sitting in the car. Thinking that this was just the latent shyness in his personality surfacing, I was a bit irritated because I felt he was being rude. To express my displeasure, I ignored his summons and continued visiting. He sent for me several more times. Ready to tell him just how impolite he was being, I finally stalked to the car. It was then that I discovered he was in no shape to visit. When he stooped over to put the groceries in the trunk, his pants had split from zipper in front to the belt in the rear.

I learned two important biblical lessons that night:

1. Giving to others is a great way to express thankfulness.

2. *Do not judge, or you too will be judged.*
Matthew 7:1

Read Matthew 7:1-6 and Psalm 92.

Pray today thanking God for his immeasurable blessings; also pray that He will give you a spirit of patience in dealing with people and will replace any judgmental spirit that you might have as well.

75.

Male Strippers Must Be Banned

Our little town had more than its share of sleazy bars. One in particular was known for its female dancers and strippers. One Wednesday night one of our dear deacons, very troubled, came to my husband. He said, "Preacher, we've got to do something as a church. Did you know that they are bringing in male strippers to the lounge this weekend?"

My husband chided him a little. "Haven't they had female strippers there for some time now?"

"Yeah, but this is different; it's a disgrace. Women will actually go see those men naked," he replied.

Although my husband pointed out that perhaps this was a double standard, the community churches did complain to the city council and stopped the male strippers from performing.

Jesus shocked the people of His day by teaching God's equality toward all men (and women). He called both Jews and Gentiles to repentance.

. . . He causes his sun to rise on the evil and

the good, and sends rain on the righteous and the unrighteous. Matthew 5:45
Read Matthew 5:38-48.

Pray that you will see others through the eyes of Christ and will realize that He died for all mankind, not just for people like you.

76.

You Told 'em, Preacher

I think all churches have at least one woman who has enough tongue for ten mouths. In our first pastorate, we had one such member. She would gossip about anybody and anything. Even if we had visitors, she would gossip that she thought they must be up to no good and that she thought they were coming to cause trouble. Having had just about enough of that kind of behavior and attitude, my husband, in his inexperience, decided to preach to *her* one Sunday. He took his text from James' teachings about the tongue, just knowing she would see the error of her ways. To his dismay, as she was leaving that Sunday, she shook his hand, told him what a wonderful sermon he had preached, and said, "Preacher, you really told 'em today. They really needed that sermon."

He learned a valuable lesson through that experience—not to target a particular individual with a sermon and that his teaching was actually one that we all need to ponder. James teaches that a person with true faith will have control of his tongue.

Humorous Happenings in Holy Places

We all stumble in many ways. If anyone is never at fault in what he says, he is a perfect man, able to keep his whole body in check. James 3:2

Read more admonitions about controlling the tongue in James 3.

Pray that God will give you control over the words that come from your mouth. Ask forgiveness for any hurtful thing that you may have said this week that has offended someone.

77.

And the Two Shall Become One

Normally, when we think of people being united in church, we think of a marriage ceremony. That was not the case on one particular Sunday. We had two members who were almost opposite in personality and disposition. One was the Barney Fife type and the other exhibited the poise of Queen Elizabeth. It happened on this particular day that this man sat directly behind this woman. She was very refined and polished and sat very still and erect each Sunday. Her carefully styled hair was always precisely in place. (It had to be because of the invisible hairnet that held it securely.) On the other hand, the man could not sit still. He constantly fidgeted. As the congregation was rising to sing a hymn, he caught his watch in her hairnet. Not knowing what was happening, she started fighting at whatever was pulling her hair. The harder he tried to free himself, the harder and wilder she flailed at the unseen thing behind her. Needless to say, the hymn was sung with much jubilation and laughter as members observed the fracas.

Only Christians can know joy and jubilation amid trouble and tribulations. We may not be happy about the trouble, but we certainly can experience the peace of the Lord in the midst of it. This is one of the mysteries which attract non-Christians to Christ. May we use even troubled times as opportunities to share the Gospel with others.

I have great confidence in you; I take great pride in you. I am greatly encouraged; in all our troubles my joy knows no bounds.

II Corinthians 7:4

Read all of II Corinthians 7 to discover some other confounding teachings.

Pray that God will give you joy in any trouble or tribulation you may face today so that a lost world will be attracted to the mysteries of Christ.

78.

Pillar of Salt

One Sunday night my husband was ordaining two young men as deacons. The service had been solemn and meaningful. Suddenly, a man with long, white hair and a flowing white beard entered the sanctuary, came down the aisle with his arms in the air and repeated, "I have a message from the Lord." My husband and I were the most astonished people there; the members who had always lived in the town recognized the man as one of the town drunks. He continued down to the front attempting to quote prophetic scriptures. One of our older deacons who knew the man gently escorted him over to a pew and quieted him.

The next Wednesday night before prayer meeting began, one of our crusty, retired teachers called my husband over to her. She said, "Pastor, you reminded me of a Bible character in the way you handled the disruption Sunday night."

"Oh, really? Who might that be?"

"Lot's wife—you just stood there and turned to a pillar of salt," she joked.

The sin that plagued Sodom and Gomorrah was certainly no joke, nor is the corruption of our generation. Changing all of society seems to be an insurmountable task. Only when we reach the world in the might of Jesus Christ, one person at a time, will we see a revolution. Peter truly had a message from the Lord which still applies today.

...*"Brothers, what shall we do?" Peter replied, "Repent and be baptized, every one of you, in the name of Jesus Christ for the forgiveness of your sins..." Acts 2:37-38*

Read Genesis 19 for the story of Sodom and Gomorrah and how an unrepentant civilization was destroyed.

Pray that God will give our generation repentant hearts and the desire to obey His commands.

79.

If You Didn't Know He Was a Preacher

Family friends are more precious than gold. It has been one of our greatest blessings to have a number of close ones through the years. In one of the churches where we served, there was a family with whom we had an unusual magnetism and fellowship. Our children were near the same ages of theirs, and we enjoyed the entire family immensely. Often we visited in each other's homes and even went on vacations together. One night after we had left their house, their youngest daughter was recounting the fun we had all experienced that night. She looked up at her mother and said, "You know, you wouldn't know Bro. Steve was a preacher if you didn't know he was a preacher." Her mother told us later that this was the ultimate compliment from her daughter because she viewed us as ordinary people rather than "untouchables."

Jesus always made himself available to the

masses; never did He put himself above anyone socially, nor should we. He talked with the Samaritan woman, tax collectors, fishermen, and governors.

I ask then: Did God reject his people? By no means! . . . God did not reject his people, whom he foreknew . . . Romans 11:1-2

Read John 13:12-20 for Jesus' instructions to his disciples as he approached the end of His life, paying special attention to verse 20 where he emphasizes *" . . . whoever accepts anyone I send accepts me; and whoever accepts me accepts the one who sent me."*

Pray that God would instill and keep a heart of love and acceptance in you as you serve as a light in a dark world.

80.

Nursing Home Blunder

I believe that all churches have at least one member who goes the extra mile in service to other people. Bill, who was one such man, was with our choir. On a Sunday afternoon he, along with the choir, was visiting a nursing home and singing for the residents. His friendliness and amiable personality had endeared him to everyone there. As the choir started to leave to get back on the bus, a little old lady on a walker hobbled out with them. Bill gently took her by the arm and led her back inside all the while assuring her that he would come back to see her. She would try to say something, "Bu-u-t-t-t-t, bu-u-t-t-t-."

Bill continued comforting her. This process was repeated several times. Patiently Bill would take her back each time while she protested. Finally she stomped her walker and balked. She looked up at Bill and desperately shouted, "I don't live here; I just came to visit my sister, and I'm trying to get back to my car to go home."

Even though Bill's kindness was overzealous, he was without a doubt trying to live out the fruits of Christianity.

It is fine to be zealous, provided the purpose is good . . . Galatians 4:18

Read Paul's instructions to the Galatians about misplaced zeal to win people over in Galatians 4:8-20.

Pray that God will keep your motives pure and that He will keep you zealous in good works.

81.

A Gun at Church

It was the middle of revival week and people were motivated to invite neighbors and friends to the service. One man had done just that. He had found children playing in the neighborhood, told them about the pre-service hot dog supper for the children, and offered to pick them up if it was okay with their parents. At 6:00 P.M., his car was filled with these excited children. Unbeknownst to the man, one of the little boys had brought his toy pistol with him. This child hadn't been to church very much and needed more supervision than he got. He left the service several times either to go to the bathroom or to roam the building. Each time he would reenter the sanctuary from a door near the pulpit. Each time he would put his finger up to his mouth and say, "S-h-h. He would linger at the door letting the door close ever so gently until all eyes were on him instead of the evangelist. Then he would go to the second row of pews and take his seat. The evangelist was becoming more distracted and irritated with each episode.

Finally, the child was so bored with the service that he started playing cowboys and Indians. He took his toy pistol from his pocket and, in great cowboy fashion, shot at the preacher with all the proper sound effects, hid behind the pew, and then rose up and shot at him again.

Finally, the evangelist had had enough. "Would someone please come and sit with this child before he hits me?" he declared.

Proverbs 20:11 teaches, *"Even a child is known by his actions . . ."* and this one truly was. The fault was not in the child though; the fault was in his training.

Read Proverbs 22 for a variety of instructions for a good life, including a guide for bringing up children.

Pray for God's leadership in training children properly, whether they are yours or others in your care.

82.

We Never Had No "Booget"

A pastor friend of ours told of a conversation he had with one of his church members. Our friend had just started his pastorate at this very rural church and the member was expressing his likes and dislikes in pastoral styles. He was strongly criticizing the former pastor (who was a young man just out of college) for thinking he could bring that church into the twentieth century.

The old man exclaimed, "That young 'town preacher' thought he was 'sompin.' He even tried to get us to have a 'booget'(budget); we ain't never had no 'booget' at this church, and we ain't ever going to have no 'booget.'

Our friend was somewhat older than the young whippersnapper and was able to *gently* lead the church into more progressive ways.

Paul taught the church at Corinth about managing money in I Corinthians 16:2. He says, " . . . *each one of you should set aside a sum of money in keeping with his income . . .")*

Read I Corinthians 16:1-18.

Pray that God will be the master of your money and your giving just as He is in other areas of your life.

83.

Shotgun Wedding?

What wedding photographers will resort to in order to get good pictures is unimaginable. Sometimes they don't even realize what they have said or done. Such was the case in a wedding my husband performed. The week before, one of our deacons called and asked my husband to come to the hospital; his daughter was there with a bad "virus." When my husband arrived and witnessed all of the troubled faces—the deacon's, the mother's, the daughter's, and her boyfriend's—he feared the girl was much sicker than first suspected.

After his asking about her condition, the family assured him she was alright. There was an awkward silence that was finally broken by the dad. "Bro. Steve, I believe this is going to be a nine-month virus, and we wondered if you could do a wedding at our house on Saturday."

My husband said, "Sure, I would be happy to. Remember, you are trying to do the right thing, and things will look better in a few days."

Humorous Happenings in Holy Places

On Saturday the family, a few close friends, the photographer, my husband and I showed up for the "celebration" only to find an atmosphere of gloom and doom. The only one jovial in the crowd was the photographer, who had no idea of the circumstances. Trying to lighten the mood and get some smiling photos of the bride and groom he joked, "Come on now, smile. You look like someone is holding a shotgun on you." Needless to say, he didn't get the reaction he desired. He never knew why he failed so miserably that day.

Weddings are endorsed by God and should be joyous occasions. God, in the beginning, created both male and female so that they may fellowship with each other and with Him. This also provides for His plan of procreation.

Marriage should be honored by all, and the marriage bed kept pure . . . Hebrews 13:4

Read about God's plan for man and woman in Genesis 1:27-31.

Pray for all the marriages of people in your church; pray that God will build a hedge of protection around each couple to keep the relationships pure and holy.

84.

A Side Trip to Jesus

A dear pastor friend of ours once took a group on a tour of the Holy Land. While he was enlisting people to go, a woman called to sign up her mother for the trip. She told the pastor, "Mother is eighty-five, and I realize she is really old to be making this trip, but it will mean so much to her. She and my dad made this pilgrimage together when they were much younger before he died, and it has been her heart's desire to go back ever since."

Wanting to fulfill the wishes of the elderly lady, the pastor agreed to take her and watch after very carefully. She actually made the trip there quite well.

One day when the group went to the Garden of Gethsemane, the lady sat down under an olive tree and died instantly. Besides being beset with the many details involved in dealing with a death in a foreign country, the pastor had to make the call to the woman's daughter. Trying to break the news gently he said, "This afternoon your mother went to be with Jesus."

With a cheery voice, the woman on the other end of the line asked, "Did she go by herself or did the whole group go?"

Our friend said the lady must have understood it to be some side trip. He explained more directly, "No, your mother died this afternoon."

Still unshaken, the woman said, "Well, I thought she might not make it, but at least she died happy." This did little to soothe our friend's frenzied nerves as he was left to take care of the many details.

Brothers, we do not want you to be ignorant about those who fall asleep, or to grieve like the rest of men, who have no hope. I Thessalonians 4:13

For reassurance about afterlife in Christ, read I Thessalonians 4:13-18.

Pray that you will live so that death will not be something to dread, but rather will be a trip to Jesus.

85.

A Slippin' and a Slidin'

In our first church out of seminary, we had a fine young man who weighed no less than 300 pounds. His affable personality and broad smile endeared him to the entire community. He attended church regularly, but he had never accepted Christ as his Savior and had never been baptized. For our annual revival that year, my husband had invited an evangelist, who is a close friend of ours. He has a genuineness and a bit of showmanship about him that attracts some people in a way that many pastors never can. So was the case in point. One night during the revival the boy walked the aisle, made a profession of faith, and asked for baptism.

Although my husband was somewhat inexperienced in baptizing, he had taken some practical "how-to perform pastoral duties" courses and thus scheduled this boy's baptismal service for the following Sunday. On the day of the baptismal service, my husband entered the baptistery confident that he could handle this guy who doubled him in weight.

He knew what to do and had instructed the young man in ways to make the service go smoothly. The only thing not covered was socks; he hadn't told the candidate not to wear his socks into the baptistery.

As he entered the baptistery, the young man grasped my husband's arm as instructed, bent his legs slightly, and waited to be taken back into the water. As my husband took him back, the boy's socked-slick feet shot out from under him and up to the top of the water. Suddenly my husband was dragged down by the unexpected surge of the boy's weight. Fortunately, he was able to regain his footing and lifted the boy up before they both drowned. That was a time of rejoicing, for more than one reason.

I'm sure my husband quoted to himself, *"I can do everything through Him who gives me strength."* *Philippians 4:13*

Read II Thessalonians 2:13-17 for encouragement regarding Christ's provision of another kind of strength to young Christians.

Pray that in this day everything you attempt to accomplish will be done through Christ's divine strength and not your own.

86.

I'm All You Can Afford

One of most pastors' pet peeves is for someone to say or ask something that derails his spiritual train of thought just before he enters the pulpit. So it is with my husband. On one occasion, a lady, who had a knack for getting under Steve's skin, was waiting in line to enter the sanctuary with the choir. Steve was also standing there waiting to enter. This sharp-tongued woman jested to him saying, "Boy, I wish we had a pastor like Dr. _____ (a famous TV preacher); I heard him this morning, and he is wonderful."

Somewhat irritated by her inappropriateness in timing and her attempt to embarrass him, he quickly quipped back, "I do too, but you already have more pastor than you can afford." He realized, and so did she, that many truths are spoken in jest.

The tongue also is a fire, a world of evil among the parts of the body . . . James 3:6

Read all of James 3 for instructions about taming the tongue.

Pray that any word which flows from your

mouth today will be an encouragement to someone rather than a hindrance.

87.

Put the Lord-d-d in the Bucket

Our minister of music is well-known for his down-home colloquialisms. Sometimes the choir knows exactly what he means, and at other times he catches us off guard a bit. Recently, we were rehearsing an anthem which had the word 'Lord' all through it. He admonished us about our diction. "The congregation won't know what you are saying unless you pronounce the final consonants distinctly," he corrected. We practiced putting the *d* on 'Lord' many times. Finally he urged, "Now, Sunday morning I expect you to put the 'Lord' in the bucket." Although, I think he meant for us to sing the word as we had learned it, the image he produced brought chuckles throughout the choir.

The image is somewhat like Miriam putting baby Moses in a basket to keep him from harms way.

. . . *Then she placed the child in it (the basket) and put it among the reeds along the bank of the Nile. Exodus 2:3*

Humorous Happenings in Holy Places

Read the entire chapter, Exodus 2, for the amazing story of how a mother, guided by God, preserved the life of one who was to become a great servant of God.

Pray that you would be willing to go to any lengths to preserve things holy to the Lord.

88.

Let 'er Rip, Potato Chip

A man, who was about sixty years old before he gave his life to the Lord, got a full dose of faith when he surrendered to the Lord. In fact, he became so excited over his newfound faith that he went to every meeting and/or class that was announced in the bulletin. He also went to Sunday School every week—he loved his new class. The teacher was a refined educated, gentleman who was kind to all. The new convert always arrived at least thirty minutes early and was very eager for the Word.

One morning after the teacher and the new convert, still early, had sat in class for about ten minutes waiting for other members to arrive, the convert, who sat directly in front of the teacher, chin held by his propped arms, exclaimed, "Well, let 'er rip, potato chip." This man's enthusiasm and eagerness to get a word from the Lord should inspire the rest of us to have that same eagerness.

Shout with joy to God, all the earth! Psalm 66:1

Read Psalm 66 for an enthusiastic approach to worship.

Pray that God will renew a desire for His word in your heart today.

89.

The Wrong Church

Sometimes we find ourselves trying to do the right thing in the wrong place. That's exactly what happened to an evangelist friend of ours. He was to begin a revival at the 11:00 Sunday morning service in a town where he had never been before. He had been recommended to the pastor by a mutual friend. Although the evangelist had never met the pastor in person, he had talked with him by phone several times that week working out details. He had told the pastor that he would definitely be there, but that he would be coming from another engagement and that the time would be tight.

As so often happens when we are in a hurry, traffic was horrendous that morning. The evangelist arrived at 11:03, rushed into the church as the first hymn was being sung, hastily walked to the podium, and sat down in one of the pulpit chairs. All eyes were fixed on him, including those of the pastor. This was not so unusual as people usually show great curiosity about a visiting speaker.

Before the hymn ended, the pastor leaned over and asked the evangelist "Is there something I can help you with?"

"Oh, no. I'm your revival speaker and it is so good to be with you."

"I think there must be some confusion," the pastor said. "We had our revival two weeks ago."

"Is this not the First Baptist Church of Gosha?" asked the evangelist.

"No, this is the First Methodist; the First Baptist is two blocks down the street."

Sometimes in our haste to do the right thing, we really mess things up. In trying to defend Jesus, one of the disciples was guilty of such an act in the Garden of Gethsemane when he cut the soldier's ear off.

Then one of those standing near drew his sword and struck the servant of the high priest, cutting off his ear. Mark 14:47

Read the story of Jesus' arrest and the actions of those around Him in Mark 14:32-51.

Pray today that you will neither run ahead nor lag behind in doing God's will but that your steps will be directed by the Holy Spirit.

90.

The Wrong Funeral

The 2,000+ membership church we attended while Steve was in seminary had a large staff. During staff meeting each morning, the pastor would assign each pastor duties for the day. One day the staff was responsible for sixteen funerals. The senior pastor tried to handle those which were for members who attended church regularly; the others he divided among the other guys. Of course, they had to just do the best they could since they didn't know the persons or their families.

One of the associates was a gregarious Texan who loved everybody and always made a point of knowing the people he dealt with. This usually endeared him to people. This day he had three obituary cards in his coat pocket. He gave a beautiful eulogy for one dear man, telling just how important he was to our church. A big mistake! He noticed the family's puzzled looks turning to anger. As soon as the service was over, one of the daughters accosted him and informed him, "Not only did you use the wrong name, you used the wrong sex; this was my mother, not my father!"

Much to his chagrin, all he could do was to repent and apologize profusely, ask the family's forgiveness, and then ask God for His. He then went to another funeral home and did the same funeral for the right person that time.

His desire that day was summed up in I Peter 3:11 which says, *"He must turn from evil and do good; he must seek peace and pursue it."*

Read I Peter 3:8-22 about suffering for doing good and living in harmony with each other.

Pray that God will forgive you for the mistakes you make or for offending someone when you intend to do good.

91.

A Toilet Paper Ministry

Most pastors truly have servant hearts. They will do the most menial tasks for people in need. So it was with a friend of ours. He is a good man, but by his admission, he has some hang-ups which have carried over from some childhood issues. One of his quirks is that he always wants a large supply of toilet paper on hand. He keeps a large white cabinet in his immaculate garage filled with cases of toilet paper.

Some of the church ladies were visiting his wife one day and saw the toilet paper in the garage. They all expressed that they had never seen that much except at the grocery store.

About nine o'clock one night, the phone rang. When he answered, one of these young ladies, who lived just around the corner asked, "Did I wake you, or are you still up?"

"No, I never go to bed this early," he responded

She continued, "Could I please borrow a couple of rolls of toilet paper?"

"Sure. Come on and get it," he said.

"Pastor, I hate to ask you this, but my children are already down for the night. Could you please bring it around to me?" she asked.

"Certainly. Just stay where you are."

As he related this incident to my husband, he told him, "Steve, in all my days of ministry, I have helped people load hay, have taken food to the sick, have mowed people's grass, but this is the first time I've ministered by delivering toilet paper!"

I tell you the truth, anyone who gives you a cup of water in my name because you belong to Christ will certainly not lose his reward. Mark 9:41

Read Mark 9:33-50 to discover Jesus' socially upside-down view of service.

Ask God to give you a servant's heart and to help you view tedious tasks as a privilege and service unto the Lord.

92.

You Know When You've Got It

Steve worked for a pest control company before he became a minister. While there, he worked with a young bi-vocational pastor. The man would come in totally exhausted on Monday mornings. Steve asked him why he was always so tired.

"Steve, when I preach in the Spirit, unction just goes out of me."

"What is unction?" Steve questioned.

"Well it's . . . No, it's like . . . Hmmm . . . Well, I don't know how to explain it, but you know when you've got it and you know when you 'ain't.'"

After Steve became a pastor, he understood more fully. One Sunday early in his ministry, he got to our car after having preached a strong sermon. He commented, "Boy, preaching sure takes a lot out of you."

I quipped back, "Yes, and listening to it does also."

Preaching and ministering to people are draining, both physically and emotionally. For this reason, it is of utmost importance that we pray for God's servants and provide assistance for them in anyway we can.

Jesus knew something about this draining of virtue. Luke 6:19 says, *"and the people all tried to touch him, because power was coming from him and healing them all."*

Read Isaiah 40:29-31 to learn about renewing your strength.

Pray that your energy and power will be used in Christ's service today and that he will renew your strength when you grow weary.

93.

Ouch! That Hurt!

It often seems that converts who spent many of their days serving the devil prior to their conversion have an exaggerated desire to do things in the church and for the Lord. Sometimes their desire outweighs their ability or Christian maturity. One such convert volunteered to play the part of Jesus in his church's Easter pageant.

The passion play depicted Christ's crucifixion on the cross. As the man hung on the cross, he was playing his part very well before the huge crowd, that is, until the soldiers were to hasten his death by piercing him in the side with a spear. Someone had supplied a real spear as a model for the set crew to use as a pattern in making the fake one.

In the excitement of the first presentation, the soldiers picked up the wrong spear, the real one, and actually pierced the man's side slightly. His depiction of Christ fell far short at that moment as he let out a loud curse word. Although this shocked everyone there, he made his apologies, repented, and continued his performance after his wound was treated.

Perhaps in his new studies of the scriptures he had not yet reached the passage about loving your enemies, found in Luke 6:28. It says, *"Bless those who curse you, pray for those who mistreat you."*

Read more about loving your enemies in Luke 6:27-36.

Ask God to give you the ability to love your enemies as Christ loved His. Pray today for someone who has mistreated you.

94.

A Peck on the Cheek

Our family is no different from others in our excitement during special events. Weddings are indeed joyous, especially when two Christians are joining their lives.

When our oldest son was marrying his college girlfriend, there was an unusual air of celebration because all who knew them felt this was truly a match made in heaven.

Steve Jr. was more excited than anyone. Even the pre-wedding photos proved to be fun. The photographer took a picture of the best man's holey socks. He had just returned from a mission trip in Africa. Steve said his socks looked as though he had been running through the jungles in his sock feet.

Then came the time for the family photos. The photographer posed the groom with his mother. He instructed him to lean over and give me a peck on the cheek. In his ecstasy, my son took the photographer literally. He took his index finger and pecked me on the cheek. The photographer explained that the peck was supposed to be a slight kiss, but the photographer liked the first one so much, he included it in the album.

A couple needs to follow the instruction in Proverbs 16:3 on their wedding day for a successful union. It says, *"Commit to the Lord whatever you do, and your plans will succeed."*

Even Jesus enjoyed a wedding; He chose one for the site of his first public miracle. Read John 2:1-11.

Commit all you do this day to the Lord and ask His blessings for your success in your endeavors.

95.

Are You Scared?

One spring a storm was brooding in the area. The weatherman warned people to be ready to move to a place of safety because tornadoes were likely. One of the families who attended the church of one of our pastor friends happened to live just across the street from him. There were three girls in the family, and two tended to be smart alecks.

When the rain started coming in sheets, our friend was concerned for the safety of the neighbor girls who were home alone. Thus, he braved the weather to go across the street and knock on their door. When the youngest of the three came to the door, he asked, "Would you girls like to come over to our house? There is a tornado on its way."

The precocious little girl looked up at him and replied, "Why would we want to do that? Are you scared?"

Our friend waded back to his house with the attitude of *if they perish, they perish.*

Storms of all kinds intrude upon the safe

havens of our homes. We can do little about physical storms; however, it is vital that we keep a protective wall up to guard our homes from the storms the devil can bring.

And . . . Satan himself masquerades as an angel of light. II Corinthians 11:14

Read about Jesus' ability to calm the storm in Matthew 8:23-27.

Pray that God will not only be your refuge in times of storm but that He will also be your fortress against the evils of Satan.

96.

A Late Surprise

A pastor friend of ours once received a call from a church member. "Pastor, how old was Moses when his last child was born?" the man asked.

"I'm not really sure, but I'm sure I can do some research and find out for you," he answered, somewhat perplexed. The pastor knew that this forty-two-year-old father's youngest daughter was already fourteen. "Do you have some particular reason for wanting to know?" he asked.

"Well, do you remember the exact dates of our last marriage retreat?" the man asked. "Count nine months forward and you will know the date on which our LAST child is to be born. I'm giving you advanced notice; I expect a big discount on our next marriage retreat."

Although the man was expressing great shock at the moment, he would later count this child a blessing from the Lord.

Abraham set the precedent for fathering children at an old age.

Abram was eighty-six years old when Hagar bore him Ishmael. Genesis 16:16

Abraham was a hundred years old when his son Isaac was born to him. Genesis 21:5

Although Abraham considered these children of his old age true blessings, read about his willingness to sacrifice his son in obedience to God in Genesis 22:1-19.

Pray that God will help you recognize that children are indeed great blessings from Him and that you are to bring them up according to His instructions.

97.

A Bird in Church

Do you remember when ladies dressed for church? I mean *really* dressed with gloves, hats, and spiked-heels? In the day before churches were air-conditioned, the church was always filled with such finely attired ladies. Of course, in order to get a breeze through the church back then all of the windows had to be raised.

On one particular Sunday during this time period my friend's mother sat listening intently to the preacher's sermon. As the service progressed, a bird found its way through the window and into the church. To all of the children's amazement, it circled the church, landed on a rafter, and flew again in search of the perfect perch. Finally, it found it—directly amidst the cluster of multi-colored flowers on my friend's mother's hat. The bird apparently found this spot to be just too realistic and too inviting. Strangely enough she was unaware of the intruder until her young son, my friend, started flailing his arms at her hat to scare the bird away.

Just as God provides places for birds to perch, he provides for our every need. He has provided a great fish, a lamb, water in the desert, a vine, a scorching east wind, and strength.

Command those who are rich in this present world not to be arrogant nor to put their hope in wealth, which is so uncertain, but to put their hope in God, who richly provides us with everything for our enjoyment. I Timothy 6:17

Do a Bible search today to discover the many ways God provides. Read Genesis 22:8, Isaiah 43:20, John 1:17, John 4:6, John 4:7, John 4:8, and I Peter 4:11.

Pray today that you will completely put your trust in the Lord for all you need; then thank him for His abundant provisions.

98.

How the Wave Was Invented

Several years ago Steve and I were fortunate enough to get tickets to see the Atlanta Braves play in the World Series. The stands were filled with happy, screaming fans. Occasionally, someone would start the wave—fans in one section would stand, raise their hands, and then sit down only for the next section to repeat the process. This continued around the stadium until all of the stands made beautiful human waves resembling the ocean. I thought the way the fans could spontaneously create such a vivid image was really neat. It was not until recently that I discovered where the wave originated.

A friend told me about these two totally undisciplined young boys who attended his church. Their parents had long awaited their arrival. Due to the fact that they had been unable to have their own birth children, they had adopted these brothers. Unfortunately, the new parents were ill-equipped for the antics of these two.

One Sunday the boys chose to sit on the front

pew. They were not there long until they decided a trip to the bathroom was in order. Rather than taking the usual route, they thought it would be more fun to crawl under the pews. They scooted on their bellies from the front of the church to the rear. At each pew, people would rise from their seats as the boys passed beneath them. As if this was not disturbing enough, they returned to their seats in the same manner. Perhaps that was how the wave really began.

A different kind of wave confounded the disciples as they were in the midst of a raging storm in Matthew 8:23-27. Jesus was sleeping, but the disciples knew that they needed His presence to face the storm. In the same way, parents need to realize that they need His presence in facing the challenges of rearing children.

Let's hope that these boys learned to obey the Lord as did the waves.

. . . What kind of man is this? Even the winds and the waves obey him! Matthew 8:27

Read where God likens his followers to little children and instructs them in their conduct in I John 3.

Pray that God will prevent you from leading little children astray, that you will show them the ways of God, and that you will teach them to rely on Him during stormy times.

99.

A Quick Swig in Church

I am often plagued with bouts of bronchitis, and I usually have a bad cough for weeks afterwards. Typically when I start coughing, I can't seem to stop. One particular Sunday, I was just getting over such an attack and was anxious to get back to Sunday School after having missed a couple of Sundays. We had not been in this pastorate very long, so I had not yet been enlisted to teach. Instead I was attending a women's class of which most of the members were older than me.

As was the custom, we sat in a semi-circle around the walls of the small room. We were packed to capacity that particular day, and I sat about half-way around the circle. The sweet, soft-spoken little lady who was teaching the class was well into her carefully prepared discourse when that unrelenting tickle in my throat began.

There was simply no way I could squelch the urge to cough. I really didn't want to disturb the lesson by getting up and leaving, nor did I want to drown out the teacher's voice with my relentless coughing. Just then I remembered that my cough syrup was in my purse. Thinking that I could take a swig of it discreetly was a big mistake. When I gently turned the bottle up, all eyes fixed on me. The teacher was silent and stunned. Then the ladies started with the jokes: "Why don't you pass that bottle around?" "Couldn't you wait to take a drink until you were out of church?" "We wondered why you were always so happy."

The lesson was never finished that morning, but the ladies sure snapped a mental picture of me that has lasted until this day. They still tease me about the "cough syrup caper."

Although we have enjoyed great fun over that episode, alcohol abuse is no laughing matter. It has destroyed countless families, ruined scores of finances, and stolen the character of many people.

The Bible's teachings are clear on the subject.

Do not get drunk with wine, which leads to debauchery. Instead, be filled with the Spirit. Ephesians 5:18

Read all of Ephesians 5 to learn how to live a life that imitates Christ.

Pray for the families you know who are struggling with drug and alcohol abuse.

100.

Why Did You Quote Mickey Mouse's Dog?

When my husband and I attended Samford University, a Southern Baptist College in Birmingham, Alabama, we lived in the married students apartments. There were sixteen units filled with aspiring preachers and their families. The guys went to churches all over North Alabama preaching. Some had their own part-time pastorates, some filled in when a pastor needed to be away, and some went out on what were known as H-Days. H-Days (which were named after the university's previous title—Howard College) had been established during the early days of the college and were days where the Baptist Association in each county of Alabama invited the young preacher boys to their churches to let them preach.

On Mondays the guys and their wives would gather informally in the yard to swap stories of their weekend experiences. On one of these occasions one of our neighbors, who had preached at an H-Day in a church located in a college town forty miles away recounted, "I studied for this sermon all week. I knew there would be professors and other very educated people in the congregation. I had three strong points, each supported with academic quotes, and I even included a beautiful poem in the conclusion."

"Well, how did it preach?" asked one of the other guys.

"It felt good, it felt solid, and I held their attention, but Patty (his wife) had a strange question when we got in the car to come home. She asked me why I quoted Mickey Mouse's dog. For my Plato quote I mistakenly said, 'And as Pluto once said . . . '"

Even though each of these guys could no doubt match this with stories of similar blunders they had made, those experiences were invaluable. The men learned to speak to all kinds of congregations, they learned what worked and what didn't, but most of all, they learned to prepare the best they could, but then to rely on the Holy Spirit, not on their own strength.

But when he, the Spirit of truth, comes, he will guide you into all truth. He will not speak on his own; he will speak only what he hears, and he will tell you what is yet to come. John 16:13

Read John 16:9-16 for more assurance that the Holy Spirit will work through you.

Pray today that you will rely on the Holy Spirit to guide you in all truth and in all your work for Him.

101.

Flicking the Bic

A young lady in one of our former churches was very industrious. She wanted a larger, more elaborate church wedding than her parents could afford. Not wishing for her wedding to be a financial burden to her parents, yet still wanting her wedding to be a dream come true, she saved most every penny she made from her part-time job for two years. She bought fabric and sewed her own dress, as well as the bridesmaid's dresses. She also bought and arranged the flowers and rented the containers and accessories.

She had chosen a yellow motif and had carried it out, even to the extent of renting a yellow tuxedo for the minister (my husband). The groomsmen had also rented yellow tuxedos. Apparently they had never attended a church wedding before. During the rehearsal, they had listened closely and had tried to carry out the instructions of the wedding director. As is customary, they weren't asked to actually light the candles at the rehearsal but merely to practice bringing the candle lighters down the aisle and fake the lighting.

The next day, the guests arrived to see a beautifully decorated church. The music began and, at the appointed time, the groomsmen proceeded down the aisle to light the candles. Because they didn't know to keep the wicks pushed up on the lighters, the flames went out before they reached the candles. In the solemnity of the moment, the groomsmen were at a loss for what to do. They were unaware that the wicks could be pushed back up to be relit. Finally, one of the young men came up with a solution, albeit a funny one. He remembered his Bic lighter was in his pocket. He took it out, lit it, and proceeded to light each of the candles with it. His hand would get hot after a bit, so he would stop the process, blow on his burning hand, and then go to the next candelabra. By the time all the candles were lit, the congregation had enjoyed a good laugh.

This brings to mind the story of another awkward situation at a wedding. At the wedding of Cana, the host ran short on refreshments. John 2:1-11 relates the story of Mary, the mother of Jesus, appealing to her son to do something about it and He did. He miraculously turned water into wine saving the host great embarrassment. Even when we think we have planned out every detail for an event, things can still go awry. Just as Mary knew whom to call on for a solution, so should we when our plans are inadequate.

When the wine was gone, Jesus' mother said to him, "They have no more wine." John 2:3.

Read this entire story in John 2:1-11.

Involve Jesus in all your plans, even before they go awry. Ask Him to direct all your activities today.

e|LIVE

---

listen|imagine|view|experience

AUDIO BOOK DOWNLOAD INCLUDED WITH THIS BOOK!

In your hands you hold a complete digital entertainment package. Besides purchasing the paper version of this book, this book includes a free download of the audio version of this book. Simply use the code listed below when visiting our website. Once downloaded to your computer, you can listen to the book through your computer's speakers, burn it to an audio CD or save the file to your portable music device (such as Apple's popular iPod) and listen on the go!

How to get your free audio book digital download:

1. Visit www.tatepublishing.com and click on the e|LIVE logo on the home page.
2. Enter the following coupon code:

   176e-abcf-96c1-2507-9281-9277-26c8-7d8f

3. Download the audio book from your e|LIVE digital locker and begin enjoying your new digital entertainment package today!